THE
REAL
LIFE
MBA

Also by Jack & Suzy Welch

Winning

Winning: The Answers

Jack Welch & Suzy Welch

THE
REAL
LIFE
MBA

*The no-nonsense guide to
winning the game, building a
team and growing your career*

Thorsons

Thorsons
An imprint of HarperCollins*Publishers*
1 London Bridge Street
London SE1 9GF

www.harpercollins.co.uk

First published in the US by HarperCollins 2015
This UK edition published by Thorsons 2015

1 3 5 7 9 10 8 6 4 2

Designed by Shannon Plunkett

A catalogue record of this book is
available from the British Library

HB ISBN 978-0-00-813789-2
PB ISBN 978-0-00-759439-9

Printed and bound in Great Britain by
Clays Ltd, St Ives plc

MIX
Paper from
responsible sources
FSC
www.fsc.org **FSC® C007454**

CONTENTS

INTRODUCTION   *vii*

PART I: IT'S ABOUT THE GAME

1   TAKING THE GRIND OUT OF THE GAME   1

2   GETTING WHACKED—AND GETTING BETTER   23

3   YOU GOTTA HAVE GROWTH   43

4   GLOBALIZATION: IT'S COMPLICATED   61

5   FEAR OF FINANCE . . . NO MORE   75

6   WHAT TO MAKE OF MARKETING   91

7   CRISIS MANAGEMENT: WELCOME TO THE COLISEUM   111

PART II: IT'S ABOUT THE TEAM

8   LEADERSHIP 2.0   123

9   BUILDING A WOW TEAM   141

10   GENIUSES, TRAMPS, AND THIEVES   157

PART III: IT'S ABOUT YOU

11   WHAT SHOULD I DO WITH MY LIFE?   177

12   GETTING UNSTUCK   195

13   IT AIN'T OVER TILL IT'S OVER   213

ACKNOWLEDGMENTS   *225*

INDEX   *229*

INTRODUCTION

Hello and congratulations—congratulations on getting it.

No, not on getting this book, although we're very happy you did.

Rather, congratulations on getting the fact that no one should do business alone.

Business is the ultimate team sport. Doesn't make any difference what size your company is, five people, or 5,000, or 150,000, for that matter. Doesn't matter if it's in Gary, Indiana, churning out steel, or in Palo Alto cooking up code. Doesn't matter if you're three days into your first job in a windowless cube about 10,000 light-years from the action, or if you run the whole enchilada from a corner office on the forty-fifth floor of headquarters.

Business is not a "me" thing. It's a "we" thing.

It's an "I'll take all the advice and ideas and help I can get" thing.

Which is where our congratulations come in. If you're reading *The Real-Life MBA*, we figure you're with us on this one. When it comes to business, you can never stop learning. Business is just too vast, too multifaceted, too unpredictable, too tech-driven, too human-driven, too global, too local, too *everything* to ever be able to say, "Been there, done that." For goodness' sake, we're still learning, and between us, we've been in business for a combined 81 years, with the last ten being the most mind-expanding of all.

Yes, the last ten have been the most full of learning for us, and here's why. After our last book, *Winning*, was published in 2005, we hit the road, launching a decade of speaking, writing, teaching, and consulting that has brought us inside scores of companies, each one facing fascinating marketplace and management challenges. We've worked with an entrepreneur in China building a firm to link foreign companies and local manufacturers, a winery in Chile transitioning away from family-owned leadership, and a young aerospace venture in Phoenix in the midst of figuring out when and how to go public. These experiences, and many more, have been windows into the nitty-gritty trials and opportunities of business in today's world. At the same time, our speaking engagements to upwards of a million people, mainly in Q&A sessions, continually allow us to hear what businessmen and women are really thinking—and worrying—about. Add to that the work that one of us (Jack) has been doing in private equity and advising CEOs since 2002, evaluating, guiding, and growing dozens of companies, in industries ranging from health care to water treatment to online dating. Finally, it was in this period that we successfully launched our own online MBA, the Jack Welch Management Institute at Strayer University, now 900 students strong. Their richly varied experiences as working professionals around the world have broadened, deepened, and informed our understanding of business today in new and exciting ways.

If we knew something about business when we wrote *Winning*, the fact is, we know more now. More that's relevant. Because business has changed, and we've been lucky enough to be in the thick of it. That's not to say what we've learned in the past decade has negated the principles and practices of *Winning*; quite the opposite. But what we've learned since 2005 has expanded, updated, and augmented them, in some cases just a bit, and in others, radically.

Indeed, these are radical times. They're *exciting* times. Sure, in some ways, it's more challenging than ever to do business. That's undeniable. The economy today isn't growing as it once did, to put it mildly; governments everywhere are more intrusive; global competition is fiercer every quarter; and technology just keeps propelling things forward faster and faster and faster.

At the same time, we're in an era of dazzling innovation. Not just in terms of cool new products and engineering processes, which seem to improve every time you blink, but in terms of how companies and people get work done. Back in 1925, President Calvin Coolidge famously said, "The chief business of the America people is business." Today, nearly a century later, we'd jigger that quote to read, "The chief business of the world is business." Practically everybody, practically everywhere, is making something, selling something, creating something, building something. This is the era of perpetual entrepreneurism, personal and professional, in organizations both small and massive, in economies old and brand-new.

Stand still at your peril. Or to be more precise, stop learning at your peril.

Better yet, embrace learning, and watch what happens to your organization, your team, and your career. Excitement. Growth. Success.

Our hope and intention is that *The Real-Life MBA* will be a part of that embrace. A big part, actually; a very current, highly useful, immediately applicable part.

You might want to use this book to supplement the MBA you're getting right now, either at a traditional campus or online. But this book is actually for anyone and everyone who is looking for a down-to-earth, no-BS primer on the big ideas and the best learn-it-today, apply-it-tomorrow techniques of an MBA. You may have already finished business school, for instance, but there's some dust on your diploma. Or you may be in a place in your life where suddenly knowing about business matters. Your first job out of college. Your first promotion to boss. Your first managerial role at a nonprofit. Your first day as CEO—and employee No. 1—of your own start-up. (Go for it!)

This book, in other words, is for anyone who doesn't want to do business alone.

Now, does *The Real-Life MBA* contain *everything* you need to know about business? Of course not. We urge you to learn about business from every possible source: colleagues, bosses, TV, websites, newspapers, conferences, podcasts, and, yes, other books. Find experts in your industry that you respect and follow them.

Find experts in your industry you disagree with and pay attention to them, too.

Our goal here is not to make you into a functional specialist of any sort. Our goal is to codify the business of business today, to give you a framework for understanding what business is about now, and how the game is played, no matter what industry you're in or hope to enter someday.

To that end, *The Real-Life MBA* opens with a section called "It's About the Game." Its chapters explore the ways in which companies, no matter what their size or type, should organize and operate to win in the marketplace: how they can get everyone aligned around a mission and behaviors, for instance, create strategy that never gets stale, rebound from a competitive drubbing, galvanize growth even in a slow-growth environment, and impel innovation—not just among the big brains in R&D, but among everyone. The first section of this book also takes a look at how to think about marketing and finance, two subjects that generate a lot of sound and fury and a big dose of anxiety, but definitely need not. And finally, the "It's About the Game" section of *The Real-Life MBA* talks about how to deal with one of the realest parts of real business today: a crisis. After all, almost no one can avoid the #RomanColiseum of public opinion anymore.

The second part of this book is called "It's About the Team." It contains our new model for leadership; it's just two imperatives, each one incredibly hard to implement yet incredibly necessary. We've also found this model to be incredibly transformative at the companies that have adopted it. Also in this section of *The Real-Life MBA*, we describe what's involved in building what we call a "wow" team, covering the blocking and tackling of hiring, motivating, developing, and retaining your best players. Keeping it real, this section concludes with a chapter that looks at managing and working with "geniuses"—that is, people whose work you couldn't do yourself, a growing phenomenon in this ever more high-tech, high-brain, high-expertise world. It also examines managing and working with people who are someplace you're not. By some estimates, 20 percent of all professionals work remotely, and the number is only growing. That doesn't make it easy or productive; we look at the practices that can make it more so.

The Real-Life MBA ends with a section called "It's About You," which focuses on career management. One chapter helps you answer the question "What should I do with my life?" Another examines, "How do I get out of my career purgatory?" And the last explores what you should do after you're officially done with your career. You will probably not be surprised to see that our answer is not "Retire."

We acknowledge that career management isn't part of a typical MBA curriculum. But in general, we wrote *The Real-Life MBA* to reflect what people in business really think, talk, and worry, about. What keeps them (and maybe you) awake at night. What gets them going in the morning.

Doing business smarter. Doing it right. Doing it so it's really fun. Doing it so it's growing, and people's lives are getting better. Doing it with a team. As in, not alone.

Business, to repeat, is a team sport.

Thanks for putting us on yours.

PART ONE

IT'S ABOUT THE GAME

1. TAKING THE GRIND OUT OF THE GAME

A few years ago, the two of us took a trip to Las Vegas. Not to play the tables; that's not our thing. No, we were in Las Vegas to speak to the International Council of Shopping Centers, 60,000 members strong.

It just so happened that the speech was early in the morning, so we arrived the night before, and with an open evening, like good tourists we decided to get tickets to a show. A famous singer was in town, and so off we went, one of us being very enthusiastic, the other being very accommodating.

Cue the 50-piece orchestra and the colored smoke machines. What a production. Big hair, power ballads, backup singers dangling on wires from the ceiling, and an eye-popping procession of costume changes.

Yet, less than an hour in, one of us was fast asleep.

Rattled awake, here's exactly what he said:

"What's the score?"

That, in three words, is a person who loves sports—and business.

They're the same thing, aren't they? Both are intense and full of fun. They're hard; they're fast. They're a nonstop grapple filled with strategy, teamwork, nuance, and surprise.

And in sports and business alike, the players are in it to win.

A brand manager wallows with his team about how to position a product out of engineering that just might blow sales through the roof. Three friends from college ditch Wall Street to start a microbrewery or launch a new app. A manufacturing manager wakes up one morning with a great idea about how to increase yield at his factory. An HR executive interviews six candidates for a job that should have been filled three weeks ago and, at last, one seems perfect.

People work all day, every day, trying to make their organizations and lives better. Trying to help their families, their employees and colleagues, their customers, and the communities where they operate.

And in working, people give their lives meaning. Not all of its meaning, of course. Life, with its vast depth and richness, certainly exists outside work. But work can give our lives a goodly portion of its purpose.

Which is why it's such a terrible thing when companies or teams are stuck in work situations that are buzzing with sound, action, and (occasionally) fury, signifying nothing. Nothing, as in no forward motion, no growth, no winning. Not even a decent shot at it.

That's not competing. That's not fun. That's not business. That's just a grind.

Such a dynamic is, however, all too common. As we mentioned in the introduction, we've spoken to about a million people around the world since 2001, almost exclusively in Q&A sessions. These individuals have worked at companies large and small, old and new, in heavy industry and in gaming, retail, and finance. They've been entrepreneurs, senior executives, MBA students, and individual contributors. Across all these varied sessions, several people in the audience usually ask something like, "Why is it so darn hard to get everyone on the same page?" or describe a work scenario where so many people don't seem to be playing on the same team, with results beginning to show for it. More evidence, too: probably a third of the nearly 1,000 MBA students in our business school, most of whom are in their thirties and forties and working in managerial jobs at good companies, report experiencing some sense of gridlock at work.

What a mess. And yet, this dilemma is not only fixable, it can be prevented.

All it takes is alignment and leadership.

They're equally important; indeed, we'd assert that neither can really happen without the other.

And there's no better way to start *The Real-Life MBA* than by digging into both.

ALL ALIGNMENT, ALL THE TIME

Now, we understand that the importance of alignment is not going to be news to most people reading this book. The concept has been out there in the management stratosphere for a long time, lauded by gurus, professors, pundits, and consultants alike.

The problem is that, in reality, at companies of every ilk, the relentless application (and discipline) of alignment can fall by the wayside.

Work—that infernal to-do list—gets in the way.

We get that. Work feels like it should come first, especially in today's daunting economic environment. A cranky client, an employee who needs coaching, a competitor's new technology hitting you blindside, a PR disaster erupting on Twitter. All these can happen in a day's work, and sometimes even on the *same* day.

But the fact is, if you want to get off the grind, alignment has to come before, during, and after "the work." It has to be happening all the time. It has to be part of what "the work" is.

All of which begs the question, the alignment of *what* exactly?

The answer is *mission*, *behaviors*, and *consequences*.

Mission pinpoints an organization's destination—where you're going and why, and equally important if a mission is to succeed, what achieving it will mean for the lives of each and every employee.

Behaviors describe, well, behaviors—the ways in which employees need to think, feel, communicate, and act in order to make the mission more than a jargon-laden plaque on the wall gathering dust and spawning cynicism.

Consequences put some teeth into the system. We're talking promotions and bonuses (or not) based on how much employees embrace and advance the mission and how well they demonstrate the behaviors.

Maybe these elements sounds obvious to you; as we said, this is not a new topic. Or maybe just the opposite. As we also said, true alignment's a rarity.

Either way, we can assure you of one thing: When alignment happens, there's no more running in circles. There's progress; that's what happens when grind gets out of the game.

ALIGNMENT IN ACTION

Without doubt, stories about alignment's transformative power can be found in every industry, but none offers quite the treasure trove of examples as private equity. Think about it. Any business of interest to a private equity (PE) firm is almost by definition undervalued. It's suffering from bad leadership or caught up in a changing market; it's a family business without a succession plan, or a corporate division that's simply been neglected, orphaned by its successful parent company. In each case, the organization is sputtering.

Now, it does happen that PE firms do get lucky, find a hidden jewel, polish it up, and get out fast with a big gain, or they buy an existing winner from another PE company, which has to sell it to satisfy the financial expectation of its investors. But those cases are in the minority. In the majority of cases, PE firms acquire the struggling business and set about doing the hard work of finding good leaders, and, almost invariably, their first and most important job is getting alignment straightened out.

Take the case of the Dutch conglomerate VNU.

Back in 2006, VNU was closing out a decade of decent, although hardly spectacular, results. In his annual letter, CEO Rob van der Bergh said he was pleased with the company and described VNU, which owned properties such as *Hollywood Reporter* and the Nielsen ratings company, as "healthy." Private equity, however, saw untapped opportunity, and a consortium of six firms swooped in and bought it up for $12 billion, hiring veteran business leader Dave Calhoun as CEO.

With a stellar career that had landed him as vice chairman of GE at age 45, Dave had managed many large businesses, but nothing like the morass of brands and products he suddenly found himself running. "When I got there, the mission was, 'We're the leader in market intelligence,'" Dave recalls. "That sounded good, but what it meant in practice was, do your own thing in your fiefdom. There was no sense of overall meaning."

Dave and his team immediately set out to change that. They dropped the name VNU, reclaimed the name Nielsen for the entire company, and made it clear that Nielsen—the new Nielsen—existed for one coherent purpose: to measure what consumers watched and bought. Nielsen was going to be the best company in the world at knowing everything about consumer viewing and buying habits all over the world.

Exciting, right?

The best missions are like that: aspirational, inspirational, and practical.

Aspirational as in, "Wow, sounds amazing—I love the idea of trying to get there."

Inspirational as in, "Great—I know we can do that if we stretch and try."

Practical as in, "OK, sounds reasonable—I'm going to work with my team to get it done."

And here's the kicker. Remember how we said well-wrought

missions let each and every employee know what's in it for them? Nielsen's nails that challenge. It promises growth—product growth, services growth, global growth—and all the career opportunities that come with it.

Another quick but illuminating mission-making example from PE is Nalco, the diversified industrial company that was bought out in 2007. In 2008, its new owners hired CEO Erik Fyrwald, who inherited 12,000 employees, $4 billion in revenues, strong cash flow, negligible growth, and a mission that could have been paraphrased as, "We're in the water business, that's nice."

Erik spent his first 90 days traveling to Nalco business units and its customers, seeking the company's killer app, if you will, a way in which to spark change and build a competitive advantage.

To his surprise and delight, he found it in a product that Nalco had developed six years previously, a water usage quality optimization system called 3D TRASAR. About 4,000 units were already being commercially leased, and Erik soon discovered that their customers loved them, passionately describing to him how the Nalco product saved water and helped prevent EPA fines like no other product.

Erik brought the news back to his leadership team, and, invigorated by the 3D TRASAR's promise, they decided to set a goal of 20,000 leased units within two years. That ambitious target, in turn, galvanized the entire organization. R&D turned its focus to improving the product's features, creating 26 patents to meet customer needs and slow any copycat competitor moves. The sales team introduced new training, goals, and incentives. At the same time, a new 3D TRASAR service center was built in India, staffed by 40 "water doctors," engineers assigned to monitor units around the world, spotting and resolving problems before customers even noticed them.

And so the company's new mission was born: "We deliver clean water to Nalco's customers in a way that makes our customers more economically successful and the world more environmentally sustainable."

Did that mission rouse Nalco to hit its goal of 20,000 units within two years? It did indeed.

"People suddenly knew why they were coming to work," as Erik puts it. "They were excited about helping our customers succeed in a way that helps save the world. They saw a future for themselves. You cannot believe the great ideas that started popping."

That's the beauty of a good mission. It gets everyone focused and fired up.

And that's when behaviors start to matter.

Matter a lot.

If a mission is a company's *destination*, behaviors are its *transportation*, the means of getting there.

We all know what this connection *doesn't* look like, right? A company spouts a mission that talks about customer focus, for instance, but in real life, its frontline employees hate customers. OK, maybe they don't hate-hate them, they just disdain them for getting in the way of what they'd rather be doing, like getting home by five. Or a company has a mission that crows about speed to market, but its managers have, let's say, a high tolerance for bureaucracy. Or a company has a mission all about delivering innovation, but the people who run things demote or fire anyone who takes a risk and fails.

Not good.

Good is when the alignment between mission and behaviors is seamless. In a company with a mission about customer focus, employees ooze empathy. They hand out their cell phone numbers so they can be reached after hours. They take complaints about poor service personally. If they had their druthers, they'd go home with every product and try it themselves to make sure it was working perfectly.

Maybe we exaggerate a bit, but you get what we mean. Mission and behaviors have to be two links in the same chain.

Now, if you've ever read our books or columns, you may be wondering at this point why we keep using the word "behaviors" instead of "values." After all, for about a decade, we've invoked the word "values" in the same context. "Values" was, you might even have thought, our favorite word.

It was. But we've found "values" can be a confusing word. It's too abstract. Too often, people hear "values" and they think you're talking politics or culture, as in "family values."

No.

Plain and simple, we're talking about how people *behave* at work and how their *behaviors* bring the company's mission to life. So "behaviors" it is.

And, to return to the topic at hand, the only reason to talk about behaviors at work is that leaders need be very public, very clear, and very consistent about what kind of behaviors are needed in order to achieve the company's mission.

Back to the Nielsen story. Right after Dave Calhoun announced Nielsen's new mission, he also announced the three behaviors that would make it come to life. The first was open-mindedness.

That was a change, to put it mildly. "People thought we were a market research company," Dave explains, "and what kind of people succeed at a market research company? Really smart people who perfect their algorithms and don't want anyone to see those algorithms because they could steal them.

"But if we were going to dominate the space of knowing everything about the consumer, we needed people who were open to data from every source and willing to work with everybody, not just the people who understood their algorithm."

The second behavior was a passion for integration. Nielsen's growth lay, Dave believed, in its people loving—not liking, *loving*—the process of mixing, matching, and synthesizing market research coming at them from every angle, largely thanks to the explosion of big data.

Growth also lay in Nielsen's capacity to make sense of all this information for their clients, and so the third behavior identified to drive Nielsen's success was simplicity.

"The digital world is getting overwhelming; all the data out there can just about drown you," Dave explains. In such situations, people often find a way to argue two sides of a case. That just muddies the waters for everyone. "If we can make a recommendation to a client in a simple, understandable way, and with conviction, we will always win." (And win they certainly did. Over Calhoun's six years as CEO, the company's market capitalization tripled.)

Erik Fyrwald and his team at Nalco similarly established the key behaviors necessary to drive the company's new mission. The first was a crusading passion for saving water. Not an "Oh, that's kind of cool" kind of passion, a "Can I tell you what I do at work? I save the world by conserving water" kind of passion. "We wanted people who got really excited every morning when they turned on their computers and saw their meters," Erik explains. And by that he means the meters all over Nalco's intranet that constantly showed how much water the company was saving cumulatively and per customer.

The second behavior was a hunger for growth. Not single-digit growth, either. Nalco's mission, Erik determined, called for growth junkies, people who saw opportunity with customers previously considered out of reach and in markets that scared everyone else away. In 2009, when most companies in Nalco's space were backpedaling in China for fear of its economic deceleration, the company brought in a strong, proven growth leader to run Asia. He moved the company's headquarters from cozy Singapore and built a new building in Shanghai, complete with a customer and employee training center, a technology hub, and sales and marketing facilities. Employment jumped from 200 to 800, with Nalco's increased commitment enabling them to recruit outstanding candidates, Chinese engineers who wanted to improve the environment through water treatment and productivity in the heavy manufacturing industries.

Around the same time, Nalco also unleashed its oil and gas unit to aggressively pursue global growth in water-related chemistry applications. (To get a barrel of oil, you also need to deal with four barrels of water to be separated, cleaned, and safely returned to the environment.) The company was quickly able to expand its business with customers doing deepwater drilling in the Gulf of Mexico, but it also moved to successfully forge new and productive relationships with customers farther afield, in locations including western Siberia, Kazakhstan, Azerbaijan, Nigeria, Angola, and Malaysia. "Our oil and gas leader was an incredible role model of entrepreneurship and pursuit of growth," Erik notes, "and he got his team to feel the same."

Clearly, his example, and that of many other believers within the organization, took hold. By 2010, Nalco's revenues and earnings were both growing in the double digits.

MAKING IT REAL WITH CONSEQUENCES

With mission and behaviors in place, all that's left for alignment is the piece of the system we're calling "consequences." Maybe that sounds punitive, but it isn't. Sure, consequences can be negative, as in demotions or removals. But far more often, consequences can be positive, as in raises and bonuses. Either way, though, our point is the same. You can huff and puff and holler all you want about mission and behaviors, but if there aren't organizational mechanisms to reinforce them, you're like the proverbial tree falling in the forest.

No one hears you.

Now, the loudest *negative* consequences mechanism, obviously, is letting people go. Most leaders hate using this tool, and they should if they're normal human beings, but sometimes when there's an obvious mission or behaviors disconnect, it's necessary and best for both parties.

Dave Calhoun, for instance, had to let go of a very popular

member of the VNU old guard who didn't think the company should or could integrate. Did he enjoy it? Of course not, but he did the right thing by making the manager's exit a teachable moment. Instead of saying, "So-and-so retired to spend more time with his family," he publicly addressed the decision at Nielsen's annual meeting. "I had to make it clear which behaviors were unacceptable and which were rewarded," he says.

Similarly, as he drove home the mission-behaviors linkage at Nalco, Erik Fyrwald had to deal with an army of resisters. "That's been tried here before, and it doesn't work at Nalco," was a common refrain. Here again, many top leaders had to be asked to move on—more than half of the top 100, their replacements drawn from internal and external candidates. Like Dave Calhoun, this was hardly Erik's favorite part of the turnaround, but a coach can't be pleading for buy-in from entrenched naysayers in the middle of the game.

The point is, when it comes to whether (and which) behaviors matter: a personnel move speaks louder than a hundred speeches.

Of course, personnel moves can also be an entirely positive form of consequence in the alignment process. The promotion of people who demonstrate the mission and behaviors is a huge message, and a great source of encouraging reinforcement through the organization. The same is true of outsized bonuses. Money talks; does it ever.

Most often, however, the consequences part of alignment is simply a matter of having a good performance appraisal and reward system in place.

Such a system does not have to be complicated or expensive. It just needs to touch—it *must* touch—every employee as often as possible, and at least twice a year, in conversations in which their manager tells them, in candid terms, where they stand.

Here's how you're helping us achieve the mission, and here's what you could do better.

Here's how you're demonstrating the behaviors we need, and here's what you could do better.

And finally: *Here's how your salary and bonus and your future here reflect what I've just said.*

That's it. That's the consequences part of alignment. How hard does that sound?

Not very, and yet, you already know how often it happens in real life. We're lucky if between 10 and 20 percent of our audiences raise their hands when we ask, "How many of you know where you stand in your organizations?" Some of our own grown children and their twenty-something friends, working in respected companies, have never received a single performance review. One of them got a nice raise in her paycheck and actually had to ask her boss why. "Merit," she was informed, period.

It makes us want to scream. (It made her want to scream too, for the record.)

So much lost opportunity, just sitting there waiting to be seized and turned into success. Clarify the mission, name the behaviors, and then measure and reward people on how well they demonstrate both.

These few tasks aren't easy. We'd never say that. But, look, alignment isn't brain surgery, either. Too darn bad that too many leaders avoid it like it is. You'll never have a healthy organization without it.

TACTICS, STARTING TODAY

So now let's turn to meet alignment's maker, leadership.

As we noted earlier, leadership is critical for galvanizing the kind of alignment that takes the grind out of work. You can have your car's tires all straightened out, but what good is it if there's no one to drive the car home, right? The facts are, in the vast majority of cases, fresh leadership is *absolutely insepara-ble* from the creation and installation of a stalled organization's mission, values, and consequences. They go together because they must.

Later in this book, we will spend an entire chapter on leadership. In fact, in it we will present a new, holistic model we've developed from the entirety of our experience and observation, one that defines leadership as the relentless pursuit of truth and ceaseless creation of trust.

But for now, in the context of taking the grind out of the game, let's talk about some key truth-and-trust *tactics*. Specifically, let's talk five immediate action steps. Because if your organization at any level is languishing, spinning, or otherwise not unleashing its full potential, you've got to start fixing that problem not next week or even tomorrow.

You've got to start today. Here's how.

First, Get into People's Skin

Is there anything worse than a pompous, self-important manager, marching around like a little general, barking at his assistant, acting like his only job is presiding over meetings with his subordinates or preparing for the same with his superiors? This officious, corner-office snob type was profligate back in the old days—like when Madison Avenue and Detroit were the center of the universe. These guys were a legion then, and the only time they left the comfort of their offices was to get lunch—together. You'd think they'd all be gone by now, wouldn't you? Sadly, not by a long shot. We've seen them aplenty over the last ten years, same as always, except with the added trick of hiding behind their technology.

Count also in this awful lot the milquetoast manager, so blah and blasé toward the work and the people you wonder why he or she bothers to show up every day.

It's crazy. If you want to light fire to all the good stuff happening because you're aligned, you need to get off your duff and get out there, truly getting to know and care about your people as individuals. In fact, really good leaders are like coaches who stand on the sidelines jumping up and down because they can't contain their excitement about how everyone's doing, who hug their players when they come off the court, never mind the sweat, and who know what makes each one of their people tick.

Let's even take this one step further. The best leaders actually care *more* about their people than themselves. This concept reminds us of a wonderful interview with Don Knauss, the then CEO of Clorox, which appeared in the *New York Times* not long ago. In his twenties, Don relates, he had been a lieutenant in the Marine Corps, stationed in Hawaii. One day, he says, "I had been up since five in the morning, and I was pretty hungry. I started walking to get in the front of the line (for lunch), and this gunnery sergeant grabbed my shoulder and turned me around. He said: 'Lieutenant, in the field, the men always eat first. You can have some if there's any left.' And I said, 'OK. I get it.' . . . It's all about your people, it's not about you."

What a great story! Great leaders build trust and credibility with words and deeds that prove, over and over again, in ways large and small, that they respect and honor their people.

Can that feel draining? At times, yes, especially when it's real, as it should be. But if you want your team to win, that should sound OK to you. It should sound like what you do all the time.

Second, Think of Yourself as the Chief Meaning Officer

How often do you think Dave Calhoun and Erik Fyrwald talked about mission and behaviors during their first 18 months at the helm? Every day? Try in every conversation, up and down the organization. That kind of overcommunication is essential, and not just as you're launching a change process. It's essential forever.

Leaders exist, in large part, to give purpose to their teams; to relentlessly, passionately explain, "Here's where we're going. Here's why. Here's how we're going to get there. Here's how you fit in. And here's what's in it for you."

Oh, and just as a reminder, once you're done explaining all that, you need to do it again.

Remember, your people spend more than 40 hours of every week working. If you're not helping them make meaning of that investment, you're wasting their time and their lives. Not to be scolds. But this part of leadership is daunting, we know that. Who likes to repeat things to the point of gagging? Exactly no one. But it's an essential part of engaging your people and caring for them, just as you would in any true relationship.

And one more thing. It's not just the top person who needs to be a Chief Meaning Officer. No matter what the size of company, it's every manager's job, right down to the team leader level, to create context and purpose. Think of how powerful that can be. Think of the alignment it creates.

Third, Remove Blockages from Your People's Way

Have you ever seen the Olympic sport called curling? With all due respect to the athletes who have dedicated their lives to it, it's somewhat curious, you have to admit. One player pushes a granite stone down the ice toward the goal, while three others precede him, frantically sweeping the surface with cornhusk brooms. Those players, the ones smoothing the way for the stone's speedy and accurate approach to its destination, do what good leaders do. They aggressively scrub out anything and everything that stands in the way of the stone reaching its target.

Like what? Well, like the bureaucratic nonsense that's endemic in most organizations. The rules and regulations that often exist just to make work for the people who enforce rules and regulations. We're not talking about the kind of guidelines you have to follow for reasons of the law or safety. We're talking about petty stuff that gums up progress. The CFO who says everyone gets a 2 percent across-the-board increase because it's been a tough year, performance be damned. The IT manager who's more interested in process than innovation, or in data collection more than analysis. The corporate lawyer who has a reason why almost anything can't be done.

A leader's job is to sweep away that kind of junk.

And while we're at it, to sweep away those kinds of people in every group—the action blockers, the change resisters, the process obsessives. "That's not how we do it around here." "It didn't use to be that way." Sometimes it's OK to tolerate a couple of these individuals—sometimes. They contribute institutional memory, or they counteract a strong culture of acquiescence, which is never to be desired. But most of the time, these people are nothing more than self-appointed, self-righteous scolds who drain energy and waste time. Good leaders know the difference, and effectively use their brooms to prove it.

Fourth, Joyfully Demonstrate the "Generosity Gene"

A scientist would have to tell you if there really is a DNA marker for generosity or whether it's more of a learned behavior, but it doesn't make any difference to us. We just know that the best, most effective, most awe-inspiring leaders share one pronounced trait: They love to give raises. They're thrilled to see their employees grow and get promoted. They celebrate their people in every way they can—with money, more responsibility, and public praise. And it turns them on to do it. We know of a manager, for instance, who was working closely for weeks with one of her employees on a project. It wasn't going well; even after hours of coaching, the employee couldn't deliver what the manager was expecting. Then one morning, the employee came to work dragging. "I was up all night," she told her boss; "check your email." The boss did, and there, in an attachment, was the project completed to perfection. The boss burst out of her office, calling out, "You did it, you did it!" for everyone to hear. That kind of drop-the-barriers, authentic generosity of spirit from leaders unleashes people to feel great about themselves and do great things for the team and for customers.

Sometimes people ask us about the prevalence of the generosity gene. That's a hard one. Personally, we've seen it, but then again, we've worked in and with some excellent companies, which tend to attract, enable, and reward this leadership behavior. In the big picture, we'd say it's probably less common. Too many leaders like to hold back on raises and promotions; they're cheapskates by nature or nurture, both financially and emotionally. They often hide their best employees to better the impression of their own performance. We have a friend, for instance, who quit a big media company out of frustration with her pace of advancement. It was only at her exit interview with HR that she learned her boss considered her a "superlative high-potential."

This manager wasn't critical of our friend, but he wasn't expressive, either. "I don't think he ever said one nice word to me," she told us. "And when I got my annual raise, it was without explanation. I didn't even know that it was the biggest in the company until HR told me on my way out the door."

It could be our friend's experience is the norm. We hope not, because nothing unleashes performance and commitment like unleashing the generosity in a good leader's heart—as well as their wallet.

And Fifth, Make Sure Work Is Fun

Can we be completely exasperated for a moment and ask, "What is wrong with people when it comes to fun at work? Really, what?" That is, why do so many—too many—assume that work is only work when it's hard, grim, dull, or otherwise unpleasant?

It kills us.

Work is not something you do while you're waiting to live. Work *is* life. Maybe not all of it, as we said earlier, but a lot of it. And that's why, if you're a leader, permitting a workplace to be a bastion of "quiet desperation," as Henry David Thoreau so famously put it, is awful. Forget about how detrimental it is to productivity and results (which it is).

Hello, fun is great. It's healthy and energizing—for organizations and individuals alike. We bet 99.9 percent of all managers would agree with that, too—in the abstract. But then, some number of them—again, too many—get to the office and suck the fun out of the place. Some do it with their negativity or lack of candor or politicking. Some do it because they think fun isn't serious, and work needs to be serious. Some do it simply because they don't realize that fun is their responsibility.

It is. Your people give their days (and sometimes their nights) to you. They give their hands, brains, and hearts. Sure, the company pays them. It fills their wallets. But as a leader, you need to fill their souls. You can do that by getting in their skin, by giving the work meaning, by clearing obstacles, and by demonstrating the generosity gene. And you can do it, perhaps most powerfully, by creating an environment that's exciting and enjoyable.

How? The options are numerous and many are wonderfully easy. Celebrate milestones and small successes. Embrace humor and candor. Let people be themselves. Smite bureaucratic behaviors every time they creep in. Banish jerks. Do stuff together outside the office. Whoever said bosses and employees shouldn't be friends was crazy. Why wouldn't you want to be friends with the people you spend all your time with?

Look, we know work has its moments of difficulty and stress; of course it does. But a leader cannot let that be the status quo. Even in the hard times, work has to be a place where people want to be. Making it so is part of what leaders do.

At the beginning of this chapter, we made the point that private equity provides a storehouse of examples about how companies can escape no-man's-land through the combined power of alignment and leadership.

But let's be clear: these same tools exist to transform floundering companies or divisions in every variety of business, from a family-owned restaurant to a global tech giant. Stagnation is all too common because people are all too human, and their organizations will pay the price.

We're not going to claim that taking the grind out of work is a layup. It's not. But it's certainly achievable, and probably more quickly than you think.

Alignment and leadership: put them together, and it's game on.

2. GETTING WHACKED— AND GETTING BETTER

The other day, one of us—not the one who fell asleep during the concert in Vegas, OK?—was in the garage looking for a favorite old golf club. The prospect wasn't promising, frankly, in that our garage is mainly a place where boxes go to die.

Surprisingly, however, one such box did hold the missing club. And it was just after locating it that our protagonist stood up and did a complete head slam into a shelf that was jutting out from the wall.

It was the ouch heard 'round the block, although perhaps it wasn't exactly an "ouch."

Look, getting whacked hurts like crazy. First there's the true, "I-see-stars" kind of pain. And then, right along with it, there's the shock. "How in the world," you wonder, "did I let that happen?"

It's only later, usually long after the bump is gone, that you come to say, "You know, getting clobbered actually taught me something. I won't let that happen again."

Business is full of whacks.

A major client uses your monthly update meeting to fire you while lodging a litany of complaints. The new product that was supposed to launch at 1,000 units a week sells 500, or 250, or 10. Your biggest competitor buys your second-biggest competitor, and starts coming after your best customers with their combined sales team. You learn that your secret-sauce marketing channel is going to be "retired" by your biggest digital partner in two weeks. A customer's bout of bad service in one of your stores sets off a hailstorm of hate on Twitter.

And then there's the kind of whack that's more like a wallop—the market you serve collapses because of a regulatory or natural event, or a disruptive technology outright kills your industry, or there's a staggering recession, the likes of which, say, comes 'round every 80 years.

Surprise!

Surprise—*sometimes*. In Silicon Valley, disastrous and sudden "disruptions" are so much a part of the fabric of everyday business, there's even a popular acronym for them, WFIO, which stands for, "We're F—, It's Over." Technology businesses, almost by nature, are whack-magnets.

By contrast, whacks can happen out of nowhere or with very little warning. Think of the businesses in New Orleans that were wiped out by Hurricane Katrina in 2005, or Superstorm Sandy in 2012.

But such outright calamities are rare. Far more often, we get whacked because our organization was not prepared; we didn't see something coming. A competitive threat, a cultural change, a new technology, the list goes on and on. It's as Google CEO Larry Page put it in his 2014 TED talk: "The main thing that has caused companies to fail, in my view, is that they missed the future."

Look, *why* your organization got whacked isn't all that important for our purposes here. Something bad happened. This chapter is about making repairs—about fixing things so that the organization rallies back as quickly as possible, and in the best-case scenario, is functioning in a way that makes another whack a lot less likely.

To that end, we've got six pieces of whack-recovery advice we're going to explain and explore in the coming pages.

1. Own your whack.

2. Hang on tight to your best.

3. Get maniacal about the drivers of costs, performance, and growth, using data as your guide.

4. Reinvent your strategy process.

5. Reality-check your social architecture.

6. Worry more productively.

Ready? Great. Because we love talking about these tactics. They belong at companies in the throes of recovery, and, we would go so far as to say, at *all* companies, whacked or not. Any coach will tell you the best defense is a good offense. Same's true in the game of business.

CODE (ALMOST) BLUE

If Hollywood ticket receipts are any indicator, everyone loves a good horror story. *Watching* a good horror story, we should say, because living through one is another matter.

Just ask Joe DeAngelo and his team at HD Supply (HDS). The company got its start in 1975 as a regional, California-based distributor to the building trades called Maintenance Warehouse. By 1997, it had grown substantially, and Home Depot, seeing all sorts of product synergies, snapped it up, establishing it as a division, and investing heavily in online ordering and logistics. HDS customers remained highly fragmented—plumbers, contractors, apartment building superintendents, facility managers, and the like. That fragmentation had never been a problem with the real estate market booming, however, and HDS had enjoyed a long stretch of success over the decades. (Its revenues in 2005, for instance, were around $12 billion, with earnings before interest, taxes, depreciation, and amortization [an EBITDA] of $1 billion.)

But then in 2008, HDS received two massive "body blows," as Joe puts it. First, the long-overinflated residential housing bubble burst. That was tough on HDS, of course, but the company was able to pivot to its secondary market, commercial real estate, which is typically countercyclical with residential. A few months later, though, the entire building sector went down the tubes with the recession, and HDS's revenues eventually fell by 40 percent. Just to stay alive, the company let go of 12,000 of its 26,000 employees, sold three of its business units, and shuttered a third of its branches.

To make matters worse, at the time of these events, HDS was

already in a precarious financial situation. Recently spun out of Home Depot and sold to private equity, it was loaded with debt. Indeed, for all the good PE can do rescuing and realigning companies, this is one of the industry's major downsides. Early on, its acquisitions often have limited cash flow and a heavily leveraged balance sheet.

"On the outside, everyone thought it was over for us," Joe recalls of 2008. "They were just waiting for the death certificate."

It wasn't forthcoming. In fact, even though the HDS story is about getting whacked at the far reaches of in extremis, the company's response provides a great example of our first four pieces of advice in action.

Own Your Whack

If you've ever been in an organization that's taken a hit, you know all the behaviors that immediately start to set in. People huddling behind closed doors, whispering about "who's going to go," managers scuttling between meetings with piles of binders and worried looks, not making eye contact with anyone, and general fear-and-loathing in the lunchroom. There's such internal paralysis that the main work going on, basically, is people gossiping and sending out resumes.

This kind of response to trouble is natural, because self-preservation is natural. But it's also a self-fulfilling prophecy. Distracted, frightened, depressed people can't fix anything.

HDS put a kibosh on this dynamic. There was no denial, and just as important, no blaming or victimhood-claiming.

Comments like, "Finance should have seen this coming," and "I can't believe this happened to us; we don't deserve it," were verboten. What good were they? Instead, HDS leaders adopted a massive "we're going to beat this" mentality, and rewarded those doing the same.

Such a mindset was achieved first by a constant invoking of the company's mission and behaviors. "We had to set fourteen thousand people all going in the exact same direction," Joe says. "Our mission was eight words: 'One team driving customer success and value creation.' We said it again and again." At the same time, the organization's behaviors were communicated through the acronym SPIRIT—service, performance, integrity, respect, innovation, and teamwork—and reinforced with small, spontaneous cash awards for the people demonstrating them. Importantly, such battlefield commissions, so to speak, were openly celebrated.

There's also a bit of theater to owning your whack. Take your pick at the best approach to reignite the organization—an off-site teambuilding event, an inspiring speaker—the options can get as creative as you want. At HDS, Joe chose to assign a special SWAT team to study the special attributes shared by the most famous champions in history—George Washington, Muhammad Ali, Secretariat, among others. Their findings—insanely hard work, a defeat-is-impossible attitude, and passion to be the best of the best—were touted and invoked in company meetings for two years. "We talked about the championship project findings *a lot*," Joe says. "Secretariat won by thirty-one lengths. We used that example all the time to reset how people were thinking. We wanted everyone asking, 'Is hiring that person going to help us win by thirty-one lengths? Is going to that conference going to help us win by thirty-one lengths?'"

The champion project, Joe says, "really helped stopship the pity party. It celebrated how we were going to get better, and that started with a very purifying thought. Losing was not an option."

Hang On Tight to Your Best

Far too often, when a company gets in trouble, its leadership has the knee-jerk reaction of firing people without consideration of performance. Many times this kind of willy-nilly approach happens because the company doesn't have a performance appraisal system in place, and wanting to show the board how fast they're acting and how deeply they're cutting, the leadership team takes the easy way out and tells every manager to fire 10 percent of their staff, or lower salaries by 10 percent across the board. Similarly, they offer buyout packages to anyone who will take them, and of course, too often, the highest-paid, most qualified people tend to snap them up and leave, as they get the best terms and have the best opportunities elsewhere.

Not to put too fine a point on it, but this behavior is the epitome of weak, cowardly, demoralizing management. Why on earth would you want to incentivize your best out the door and risk setting off a mass talent exodus?

Getting out of a hole is hard enough. But you are never, ever going to get out of a hole without your best people. That's why in hard times, you must do something counterintuitive and even courageous, which is give your best people *more* in current pay and long-term, performance-based equity, going so far as to err on the side of too many participants rather than too few.

We say courageous because, in the darkest days, bringing such an idea to your boss, or in some cases the board, can feel like walking into moving helicopter blades. Your boss is often paralyzed and the board is worried about proxy optics. It takes guts to say, "Let's compare our proxy noise embarrassment about pay with the pain of bankruptcy headlines, shall we?"

But guts are required. Indeed, more than guts. If there was ever a time to unleash the generosity gene we talked about in the last chapter, it is now. In hard times, your best people become your best role models. "If Sam and Sarah are staying," other employees think, "things can't be that bad and they're definitely going to get better. I'm in."

Or put another way: your best people are your best hope for survival—and success. Do what it takes not to lose them.

Get Maniacal About the Drivers of Performance

With the right people on board, you can turn to the next part of fixing your whack. That is, meticulously searching for ways to improve every part of the business.

Meticulously? Hello, that does not mean slow. It means intelligently and deliberately, and in particular, it means driven by the vast stores of information about markets and consumers now available for free or for a price. Some people refer to this new ocean of facts and figures as big data, and we suppose that's fine (if a bit jargony). For us, the imperative around big data is not necessarily getting more information; you could drown in it all.

The main issue is discerning what information matters to your organization and crunching it to determine the true drivers of cost and growth. Ultimately, it is as Sir Terry Leahy, the former CEO of Tesco, has so famously (and wisely) said: the only data that matters is the data that is actionable.

It was just such analysis that allowed HDS to quickly decide which businesses to divest because they had no clear path to a leadership market position. "The diagnostics allowed us to see what we needed to see," Joe says. "We looked at every external market. Is there a way for us to make money there? What are the customer needs, which of them is most important, and how do we compare to our competition?" Similarly, the data pinpointed the best opportunities for investment.

As a result, HDS sold off lumber, plumbing, and industrial piping, redoubling its focus on facilities maintenance and upping its technology investment to improve its delivery logistics. At the same time, again using a heavy dose of data analytics as a tool, the company launched a program to reward and spread process improvement. Its Los Angeles operation, for instance, was scoring much better results than other HDS outposts on numerous measurements. A headquarters team was assigned to find out why, and make sure its superior practices were disseminated across every branch of the organization. Meanwhile, every member of the HDS field team was hitting the streets with a new iPad loaded with Salesforce.com software, with its reams of information about which products to promote to each customer for the best results.

"We were maniacal about performance, basically," Joe says. "In a life-threatening event, you have no alternative."

Fortunately, today, due to advances in data gathering and analytics, maniacal can mean meticulous and fast at the very same time.

Reinvent Your Strategy Process

Let's move on to something else critical to HDS's recovery: the way the company handled strategy, post-whack, which for our purposes also illustrates how strategy and tactics should be increasingly integrated today, regardless of circumstances.

Because the truth of the matter is, strategy-making—at least as those of us over 40 used to know it—is dead. It's irrelevant. Big, staged biannual sessions with elaborate presentations about "trends" and "core competencies" and the like? Meetings before the meetings to establish buy-in with "internal constituents"? Forget it. Markets move too fast for any of that old ritual. They move too fast, and they *change* too fast.

Now, we've long been proponents of a much simpler, more flexible approach to strategy that we call the "Five Slides," because the process can basically be boiled down to, obviously, five slides. These slides, incidentally, should not be created by some sort of "SVP of Strategy" or outside consultants. No, they should be created by a team led by the CEO and comprise an organization's best minds, engaged, knowledgeable, curious, and original. People who are likely to debate, and even disagree, drawn from any and every part and level of the organization that makes sense. And, importantly, people with a propensity for paranoia—not just what-if-ers, mind you, but worst-casers. Strategy today demands that kind of mindset because in business today, virtually anything can happen, and it does. A tech start-up comes in the side door and topples an industry giant. An offhanded comment by a senior executive offends a huge category of customers. Oh, the list goes on and on.

Which is why the Five Slides are so paranoid and externally focused in their approach. Their objective is singular, actually, as it should be in any strategy process: to get the organization outside itself—a huge challenge! A review:

The first slide provides a nitty-gritty assessment of the current competitive playing field. Who are our competitors? What's their market share; what are their strengths and weaknesses? What does it look like inside their organizations? For the process to work, please understand that these kinds of questions cannot be debated at 10,000 feet, like some sort of white-glove, intellectual discourse. We've seen that too many times, and it's a waste of energy. You have to wallow in the detail—as if you're in each and every competitor's conference room. Does that sound hard? Well, it is, absolutely. It takes rigor and discipline to really dig into the competition's head. But if there is one thing we've seen time and again, it's that strategy-makers underestimate their competition in the present time frame—for instance, dismissively opining, "That company's crazy with their prices—they're going to go out of business," rather than asking, "Whoa, are our costs too high?" To make matters worse, they also imagine the competition as stagnant when predicting the future. Sorry, but we just can't hammer this one hard enough. People can't seem to help themselves. In their analysis, they're moving forward while their competitors are assumed to be standing still. It's nuts. The antidote can only be: when it comes to market analysis, be afraid, be very afraid.

On the second slide, you put together an assessment of all your competition's recent activity in terms of products, technology, and people moves that changed the competitive landscape. On the third, you outline what you've been up to in the same regard over the same time period. The fourth slide identifies what's around the corner, in particular what worries you to pieces, such as a competitor's new product, an M&A deal that could really shake things up, or a disruptor from another industry showing up to play in the space. And the fifth and final slide identifies what you see as your big, wow-worthy, winning move to change and dominate that same space, filled with old, new, and potential competitors alike.

The Five Slides approach obviously reflects our belief that strategy is not a particularly high-brain endeavor, but far more a matter of coming up with the *big aha* for your business, putting the right people in the right jobs to drive the aha forward, and relentlessly seeking the best practices to achieve the aha. (For the record, we define "big aha" as a smart, realistic, relatively fast way to gain a sustainable competitive advantage.)

Now, when we first started talking about the Five Slides approach to strategy about a decade ago, it was received as somewhat "outside the lines." No surprise, really, as MBA curriculums at the time (not to mention the consulting firms that employed many of their graduates) were built around the strategy-making process being as intellectually complex as humanly possible.

Over the past several years, however, we've observed a significant movement toward more flexible, swifter strategy processes that promote agility. Because being agile really matters. At a tech conference we attended not long ago, for instance,

Qualcomm's then CEO Paul Jacobs (he is now executive chairman) noted that his team conducted an informal strategy review monthly, and if the markets were demanding it, more often. No one in the audience seemed shocked by this statement, and many nodded approvingly, as if they knew exactly what he was talking about.

Which brings us back to HDS. Before it got whacked, it too wasn't exactly stuck in old strategy habits, it just hadn't fully embraced the new. But its crisis changed that, to put it mildly. Instead of quarterly strategy sessions, it moved to market reviews every Thursday.

Yes, every Thursday.

Just as significant—and this is really key—the company made sure its Thursday strategy (and tactics) review process was an exercise in exploring the external world.

Look, too often, strategy can become a bunch of people in a windowless room (literally and figuratively) talking about history. About trends they've seen. About who did what back when. About things they know to be true because that's the way they've been. About the way things just seem to go in the business. About what's happening in the company right now—as in, what it can do and can't do because of this person and that person.

No, no, no.

Effective strategy-making is about the future—and the markets. Customers and competitors today, tomorrow, and a year from now, technology coming down the pike sooner and later, products not yet invented, looming social and political events. You name it—as long as it is *out there*.

At HDS, "I just kept returning every strategy conversation to the markets," Joe says. "We were never going to succeed talking about us and what we could or couldn't do. We had to talk about the customers, the competitors, new products, new services, new technologies. What else is there?"

That's a great question.

Let's now turn to our final two pieces of advice about surviving a whacking, and, indeed, getting better because of it.

Reality-Check Your Social Architecture

Social architecture describes how a business has its people arranged—its reporting relationships—and inasmuch conveys who and what are important to the organization. Put simply, we're talking about the "org chart."

Generally, people in business avoid talking about org charts because they're boring, especially when dotted-line-heavy matrix organizations come into the conversation. Org charts can also make some people a bit frantic, especially people who care a lot about how high their little box is compared to other people's little boxes. But that's not our point here.

Our point is the following: in our experience, too many companies still get whacked because their social architecture has not changed with the times. And to be even more specific, because their social architecture is too often a relic of the past, with today's critical functions of IT and risk management reporting either to the wrong level (misunderstanding their importance) or on the wrong function (misunderstanding their value-add).

Hanging on to outdated social architecture usually isn't malevolent, of course. But it still happens, a historic habit, left over from the days when the nice semiretired lawyer or out-to-pasture accountant in risk management chatted with the company's auditing firm a couple of times a year and checked in with the line people every now and again. As for IT, well, it was the number you called when you wanted help running a WebEx with your team in the field.

Today, of course, IT has a major strategic function in just about every business. And with the rise of cybercrime and proliferation of government regulation, risk management should be as well.

Yet, in too many companies, we still observe that the social architecture doesn't reflect reality. Risk managers are trotted out to report to the board twice a year and get patted on the head and sent back to their caves. Similarly, the leaders of too many companies can't bring themselves to let the CIO into the room for strategy conversations. We certainly know where that fear comes from. Even with the advent of low-cost cloud-based solutions, it can still feel like IT comes around too often asking for huge sums of money to upgrade this or that system, or for some other "urgent" technology infrastructure project no one really understands. *"Puh-leez,"* everyone is thinking to themselves, "make your expensive gobbledygook go away."

There's a terrible cost for marginalizing risk management and the CIO, however, and the time you see it is when a company has just taken a huge whack. Take the case of Target. Right before Christmas in 2013, during the peak-peak of the year's biggest selling season, the store had the very unpleasant task of announcing that cyber-thieves had broken into its system, accessing the account information of 70 million customers.

Seventy million!

Target is hardly alone. Think of Sony's hacking debacle, surrounding its release of *The Interview*. It was nothing short of an international incident. Think of GM recalling millions of cars for lethally faulty ignition switches after 13 deaths. Think of JPMorgan Chase losing billions of dollars due to the so-called London Whale incident.

How agonizing. Disaster shouldn't have to strike for companies to examine who's reporting to whom, and how often. There is, of course, no "ideal" social architecture. There is only the "ideal" social architecture for each individual company and its market. That said, it's hard to think of a business today that shouldn't have risk and information tech positions filled with the top talent, talent that understands not just their immediate function but the business strategy as a whole, connected closely to top leadership in high-profile reporting relationships, and sitting in the room during every conversation that matters.

And Finally, Worry More Productively

Last year, we got a midnight email from an old friend. This friend, whom we'll call Julie here, runs a $2 million ad agency with a part-time staff of 12. And she's thinking of adding more, in fact; business is booming. Yet her late-night missive read, "I'm worrying constantly these days. It's stupid to worry, right?"

Wrong.

It is only stupid to worry about worrying. It's smart to worry as long as you nail down what you're worried about—and face into it.

Look, we don't need to belabor this point except to say one thing: in business, worrying can often be a signal you're about to get whacked. It's your early warning system, based on just . . . stuff . . . vague inputs. A big client taking a few hours longer than usual to return emails. Unexpectedly positive tweets about a competitor's product that you'd written off. Your landlord making noncommittal noises about his plans to sell the building "eventually."

These kinds of mushy, nebulous data points are part of every manager's day, and too often, managers wave them off. As we said in the last chapter, "the work" gets in the way. Our message there was that alignment is part of the work. And our message here is that worrying—*constructive* worrying—is too. Doing the painful pinpointing of what trend, occurrence, offhanded comment, or whatever-it-was that is causing the uh-oh feeling in your stomach, and then doing the equally painful investigation into whether your worrying is justified or paranoid. You win either way. If you discover your worry is justified, you can fix things before it's too late. If you discover you were just being paranoid, you can rest easy with the knowledge that, at least this time, you're not going to need to groan, "Damn, I knew that was coming."

Our friend Julie, unfortunately, didn't want to go there. When we pushed her to identify the source of her worry, the best she could do was, "I just get the feeling Harry is mad at me." Harry was the VP of marketing, and Julie's main point of contact, at her marquee client.

Then we advised her to visit Harry to test her concerns. She demurred. You guessed it—she was too busy.

At their next monthly meeting, you guessed it again, Julie was fired with a litany of complaints about her team's shoddy performance. We alluded to her whacking, in fact, at the beginning of this chapter.

She called us right afterward. "I'm just sitting here in my car. I can't bring myself to go back to the office and tell everyone. It's too humiliating," she said. "I'll do it tomorrow." We weren't going to suggest otherwise. Whacks, as we said earlier, can hurt like crazy.

Nor did we want to remind her of her midnight email. But she brought it up. "I told you I was worried," she said.

Yes, she had. But not worried enough to worry the right way—the way that chases worry down and catches it. After all, it's far better to own your worry than own your whack.

We saw Julie recently. Harry is gone as a client, but getting blown out the door by him that fateful day was a great learning experience. She and her company, she says, are better for it having happened.

That's the way whacks usually work.

Joe DeAngelo would agree. "I wouldn't want to do it again," he says of HDS's near-death experience, "but it allowed us to refine and hone everything we were doing. A crisis does that. It gives you the speed and the urgency to fix what's broken a lot faster."

In 2014, HDS had a very successful public offering, giving its employees and owners a great opportunity to celebrate what surviving a whack really feels like.

The facts are, a whack can hit any size company, from a multibillion-dollar conglomerate to a one-person show. That's life. That's business.

Just remember this. If one comes your way, a whack is a terrible thing to waste.

3. YOU GOTTA HAVE GROWTH

Remember the old advertising slogan, "Nobody doesn't like Sara Lee"? It became an instant classic. First, because it was so charming and catchy. But second, because on some visceral level, it made you realize how few things there were in life upon which everyone does, indeed, agree.

Growth is one of those rare topics. Everyone likes it. Especially in business, where most everyone loves it.

In fact, with the exception of a professor who once submitted an article called "What's So Great About Growth?" to the *Harvard Business Review*, we don't believe we've ever met anyone who doesn't get that growth is the elixir of life in organizations of every size and ilk. A new product, a new service offering, a big new customer—ring the bell! Things are getting exciting around here.

Now, there was a time that some of us (fondly) recall when growth was part of the natural order of things. From World War II until 2008, the economic cycle, generally speaking, had its usual ups and downs. Bumping up revenues and profits each year wasn't exactly a slam dunk in this period; global competition was robust in many sectors. But you know the old adage about the rising tide. A lot of ships, some seaworthy and some not so much, got lifted.

Then came the financial crisis. No need for a history lesson in these pages. We all know what's happened in the past several years, and we all know what it's meant for business. Growth has been tough to come by.

You can debate where the fault lies for the stagnant growth environment, but look, that's the way it is. You can't just roll over. You can only push back. Or in the case of business, you can step up. It doesn't matter if you're the CEO of a major corporation or the manager of a six-person team. When something is challenging, as growth is these days, it's your job to rally the troops.

The fact is, growth is a mindset. It's an attitude—an attitude that starts with the leader, and then gets passed through the organization, like one candle lighting the next in a darkened room, until the whole place is ablaze. Remember Joe DeAngelo, the CEO who took HD Supply out of the deep stuff to success? He puts it this way: "Every person has to come to work every day knowing you're a growth company. Growth just doesn't happen any other way. If you don't think growth every day, and say growth every day, it won't happen."

Amen to that.

And amen to the reason why. Growth is great because growth is what gives people job security, pays for a child's college tuition, buys a home, and all the while builds meaningful careers. Growth is a huge part of what makes business fun.

But how, right? *How* do you grow even in slow-growth times?

Much of the answer to that question, as you might have surmised, lies in the first two chapters of this book. Aligning mission and values. Embracing the kind of leadership that inspires performance and innovation. Maniacally crunching the data to drive performance, using fast, agile strategy-making. Installing modern social architecture. Worrying productively. Of course those activities promote growth!

So if you're starting *The Real-Life MBA* with this chapter because growth feels like it's your chief challenge, we respectfully suggest you start at the beginning.

But if you've been with us since page one, we've got some additional levers that we know to be powerfully effective catalysts for growth, six to be exact. Bring in fresh eyes. Whatever you do, don't sprinkle resources. Redefine innovation so that it's everyone's job. Put your best people on your growth initiatives. Make sure you're compensating people for the right things. And finally, co-opt growth's resisters—by any means necessary.

EYES WIDE OPEN

If you've ever endured a hospital stay, or cared for someone who has, you're probably familiar with the world of home health care. Released from the hospital though not feeling 100 percent, suddenly you're back in your own bed, loaded with instructions about how you can now do all the things the nurses were just doing for you. All you need are the supplies.

Enter a company like AssuraMed. One of AssuraMed's divisions is called Edgepark Medical Supplies, a mail order business that exists to sell you, the consumer, everything from rubber gloves to diabetes pumps, and handle your insurance claim while it's at it. Its other division, Independence Medical, sells the same products to medical supply stores, some 10,000 in number.

AssuraMed is, in many ways, the archetypal American success story. Founded in 1928 as a corner pharmacy, it expanded into the home sale of products in 1968, went regional, then national, and was logging about $4 million in revenues annually when an Ohio family named Harrington purchased it in 1990. The Harringtons continued the business's growth trajectory for 20 more years before selling it to private equity in October 2010.

Unlike many PE acquisitions, AssuraMed wasn't a mess, or even close to it. RGH Enterprises, as it was called before being sold, was profitable, with low-double-digit revenue growth. Its managers were competent and content.

Enter new CEO Michael Petras. Michael had been the CEO of the lighting business at GE, an industry where even incremental growth was brutally hard. Suddenly, all around him, he saw so much opportunity—heaps of it, just waiting to be seized. And so he fired up his team with a "faster, faster" growth message. It became, in fact, the company's new, overarching theme. It became its organizing principle and daily rallying cry.

Michael would tell you he and his team simultaneously pulled all the levers we're going to look at in this chapter. That's true. But for the purposes of discussion, let's look at them one at a time, starting with a tactic he calls "fresh eyes."

As in, "hire new people."

Don't panic. We realize that if you're reading this, you probably feel as if you've already tried everything to spur growth and pushed every one of those efforts to the wall. Your customers wanted faster delivery; you embraced lean Six Sigma techniques and cut door-to-door times in half. The advertising revenue supporting your website was contracting; you moved to a subscription model. You've added every new service imaginable; you've taken the term "best practice" to the limit. And the results have been OK. You've gotten the business up to a 2 percent real-growth top line in a 2–3 percent economy, and with a nudge from enhanced productivity, you've leveraged that "growth" into solid single-digit earnings improvements. Not what you'd hoped for, given the resources invested, but the most you could expect today.

The problem with that line of thinking is, you probably haven't tried everything. You've been too accepting of the circumstances. And to break out of that place, you need new brains in the game.

Now, when you're not growing very fast, the last thing you want to do is go on a hiring spree. You like your team, even if it's just four of you. They're experienced; they've been with you shoulder-to-shoulder, trying out new initiatives. We empathize. But here's reality: you and your team don't know what you don't know.

At AssuraMed, Michael Petras was surrounded by people who had "grown up" at the company. They knew the industry down to their toes. Michael didn't want to let them go, because like you, he knew their value, but for the sake of fresh perspectives, he moved some of them into different roles and brought in six new leaders from companies outside the medical industry, including Hewlett-Packard and Grainger. And in perhaps the most startling move, he brought in a new marketing manager from Lean Cuisine, a frozen food division at Nestlé. Her name was Kristin Gibbs, and she took one look around AssuraMed and, like Michael, saw a veritable gold mine of growth possibilities. The company had long segmented customers by product, for instance. Kristin wondered what could be learned—and improved—if they were segmented by "disease state"— urological, insulin-dependent diabetic, and so on. Similarly, she noticed the company had not aligned its marketing programs with those of its manufacturers. What would happen if it did? Nor had the company ever spent much time promoting itself to nurses. What if it started showing up at their conventions, sponsoring luncheons, and telling the AssuraMed story?

The impact of Kristin's various marketing initiatives was immediate and profound. Not because she was a new manager who introduced new managerial techniques, but because she was a new manager who saw the organization with new eyes— for what it was and what it could become.

If you want growth, no matter the size of your company or where you sit in it, be it leading a team or a department, don't delay in bringing in a pair (or two) of your own fresh eyes.

CONCENTRATE, DON'T DILUTE

Most businesses have only so much money to spend on growth initiatives each year. And most of the time, whether the budget is $100,000 or $10 million, it's not enough; again, that's just one of those facts-of-life things.

But too often, the problem with growth isn't the number of dollars available, it's how managers allocate them.

They sprinkle. A little money on this initiative, a little on that, a bit more over here, some over there, until each initiative gets a dusting of funds, and everyone is unhappy. At least they're *equally* unhappy, right? Or so goes the thinking of weak leaders practicing the age-old, favorite corporate pastime of CYA (covering your ass).

Such an approach, common though it may be, is a losing game. If you want growth, don't hedge your bets. Go big to get big. That's our second lever.

Michael Petras had lots of ways to allocate his resources toward growth at AssuraMed; indeed, within his first year, his top team (those fresh eyes again!) brought him more than a dozen investment options. They all had some merit—that was exciting. And so Michael and his team debated them for days. If you'd been there, the intensity at times would've reminded you of a good old-fashioned food fight. Ultimately, for maximum payback, they decided to fund only two. One was Kristin's segmentation initiative and associated marketing projects. The other was a significant departure for the company—pushing aggressively into the urology market, where the company had a negligible presence.

Not surprisingly, expanding the urology business was met with skepticism by AssuraMed's old guard. "We've tried that already," they said. "Our competitors have it locked up." But Petras argued that AssuraMed had never gone after urology with resources and commitment. And that's what the company did in 2012, investing heavily in leadership, a dedicated sales force, and expanded billing capabilities. By the end of 2013, the business had doubled in size.

Who'd-a thunk it? Not anyone accustomed to sprinkling.

One last thought on growth and resource allocation. As we said, it can seem as if there's never enough money to fund growth the way you know it "has" to be funded. "To get this new product off the ground, we need at least $150,000 in advertising," you might tell your boss.

"I hear you. Here's $50,000," might come the answer.

Sometimes $50,000 is all there is to spare in the budget. Sometimes $50,000 is all you get because of the sprinkling going on.

Regardless, in such situations, your only hope is to innovate around the problem. Unleash creativity instead of dollars.

Like WestJet Airlines did.

It happened like this. In December 2013, vastly outspent by competitors and facing a lack of awareness in their target markets, WestJet picked two flights traveling from Toronto to Calgary and installed a present-shaped kiosk with a digital screen in the waiting area. An interactive Santa Claus greeted customers before they boarded. Ho-ho-ho, he said, who are you and what would you like for Christmas? It all seemed harmless enough; most people were game and answered. A camera, one customer replied. Socks and underwear, said another. A blender. A warm scarf. And on and on.

The planes boarded, and probably 90 percent of the flyers forgot about their Santa encounter. But unbeknownst to everyone, WestJet personnel on the ground in Calgary were frantically shopping to fill every wish. And when 250 people landed and went to Carousel 8, instead of their luggage, they were greeted with wrapped and labeled presents.

We dare you to watch the video on YouTube without getting a little emotional. Try it; 36 million others have gone before you.

Yes, WestJet's marvelously innovative marketing Hail Mary resulted in 36 million views. We don't know how many millions it would have cost to buy that many impressions in conventional advertising, but certainly more than the company spent on presents by orders of magnitude.

Look, the facts are, there's rarely enough money for every last growth initiative. So spend what you have, spend what you can. Just no sprinkling.

ALL HANDS ON DECK

Let's keep talking about innovation for a minute more, because it is the growth driver that seems to get the most glowing press and puffy rhetoric in just about every CEO's annual report letter.

That's all well and good; hey, we just used WestJet's brilliant marketing idea as an example of innovation's power to change the game.

But generally speaking, our view is that most people and pundits in business think about innovation too narrowly, and, as a result, miss all sorts of possibilities for growth.

Here's the problem: our culture has the notion—the stereotype, if you will—that innovation is the purview of the Edisons, Einsteins, and Jobses of the world. The uber-brilliant, practically otherworldly geniuses who disappear into their labs or lairs only to emerge with an invention that changes everything.

Such rare and wondrous people do exist, of course, and thank goodness for them.

But if you want to spark growth in your organization, you need to set aside what such rare and wondrous people tell us about innovation—that it's done by lone geniuses and that it's all about big, disruptive breakthroughs. That bar is too high. It sidelines too many people, allowing them to think, "Innovation is for someone else to do, not me. I may be smart, but not that smart."

It's like quitting on your first day of work.

Listen: innovation in business is most likely to occur when it is defined to (also) mean incremental improvements that are held to be everyone's job. It can and should be a continual, ongoing, *normal* thing. It can be and should be a mindset that has every employee at every level of the organization thinking as they walk in the door every morning, "I'm going to find a better way to do my job today."

Think of what might happen then. Suddenly, innovation becomes finding a way to close the quarterly books in six days instead of eight, improve inventory turns by 5 percent a quarter, or use technology to allow calling on four customers a day instead of three. Innovation becomes a mass movement to continually improve how work gets done. And there's rarely a mass movement that doesn't have an impact.

Now, one thing about this mentality. It will not happen with a few speeches by the boss. "Innovation is great! We must have it!" To quote the great New York admonishment, *fugghedabou-tit*. People will nod and maybe even applaud, then return to their desks and get back to their real work, never to think about innovation again. No, this kind of mindset requires a culture of recognition, in which leaders celebrate the heck out of incremental improvements. Sam in the call center figured out a way to increase customer retention rates by 5 percent—time for an office party toasting his discovery, with the very public reward of two tickets to a great new show in town. Marie came up with a way to avoid downtime in the factory by a small shift in scheduling that everyone liked better anyway. Send her family to Disney World. Whatever—the details aren't important. Just celebrate in a way that feels right and makes sense. (Knowing, of course, that celebration never, and we repeat, never, means dinner with the boss. Because no matter how wonderful and fun a boss is—and a few are—dinner with the boss is still work.)

OK, that's it on this topic. Bottom line: we're inspired by epic inventors as much as everyone else. But all sorts of opportunity for growth lives in a counternarrative, and one that's equally true. You don't have to be a genius to leave a meaningful mark.

You just have to believe that incremental improvements are innovation all the same.

MATCH THE TALENT TO THE TASK

Earlier in this chapter, we made the case that when it comes to resource allocation for growth, you need to "go big." Now we want to make the case that this very same principle applies to the people you assign to growth initiatives. Make them your best. It's the only option that works.

"Of course," you're thinking, "that's a no-brainer."

It is—but it doesn't happen often enough or deeply enough.

Even at really smart companies.

Case in point: One of us recently attended an operating review at Hussmann, a midwestern refrigeration manufacturer. It's a solid business, with new, engaged leadership, recovering well from being orphaned by a conglomerate. The session was dominated by discussion of the company's major growth initiatives and their progress. Each of the initiatives definitely had market potential. Each was adequately funded. But the results were coming more slowly than everyone wanted and expected. What was going on?

One answer to that question was fascinating—and critically important for our purposes here. It came when the CEO, Dennis Gipson, who was orchestrating the meeting, had the self-confidence to turn to the head of HR, Scott Mannis. Dennis knew that Scott had done a complete analysis of the situation, and his findings pointed to a gaping disconnect between the talent level required to launch the growth initiatives and the talent actually assigned to them.

Hussmann was a company that, fortunately, had a rigorous performance appraisal system, which differentiated employees into top tier (about 20 percent of the total), average to good (the middle 70 percent), and not meeting expectations (the bottom 10 percent).

With such information, Scott was able to create a chart, which he proceeded to present to his colleagues that day. It plot-

YOU GOTTA HAVE GROWTH

ted each of the company's growth initiatives on the vertical axis, and across the top, on the horizontal axis, it plotted the categories (20-70-10) of the personnel assigned to those initiatives. The resulting chart clearly showed that not enough of the best people were populating the high-growth initiatives. Eureka.

This is a chart that every organization seeking growth—in other words, every organization, period—should live and die by. We repeat: such a chart is a game-changer. It really puts the people management process right in the middle of the action. If you want growth, you have to staff the engines of growth with your best.

Luckily for AssuraMed, an understanding of the importance of putting your top people on growth initiatives was something Michael Petras brought with him. He selected a very high-potential manager from within the organization to run the company's foray into urology. The fledgling unit needed the manager's firepower, Michael believed, but he also knew that moving and focusing a star player from the company's main business would make a huge statement to the whole company about the strategic importance of the growth initiative. Such appointments, as we noted in Chapter 1, speak more loudly than a hundred speeches.

Not surprisingly, when Michael sat down with the manager and delivered the news, he was taken aback.

"I have a better job than that right now!" he protested.

"That's true," Michael agreed, "but you're one of the best people in the organization. The new venture needs you. The company needs you."

And so it must be. Growth doesn't lead itself.

KEEPING COMPENSATION FRESH

The next growth lever is the sweat-the-details-iest. The in-the-trench-iest. The gruntiest, if you will.

It's measuring and rewarding people for growth.

Remember how in the last chapter we said that big data was all well and good, as long as you weren't letting the vast new ocean of information drown you? Our point, if you will recall, was that data can tell you lots of things these days, but its best use is helping you zero in on the actionable items that will truly drive growth and reduce costs.

The two, of course, are related. What really drives your profitability? Is it sales, margins, customer acquisition costs, or customer retention? Is it improving your product features, or long-term service contracts?

Perhaps you already know the answers to these questions. That's great; you should.

But do you then measure and compensate your people for their performance accordingly? Don't say yes without really staring this one down. Because here's the story. Performance and compensation systems go stale with time, and in today's world, with its rapid-fire technology changes, they grow stale ten times faster than ever before. So you may think your organization measures people for the right things, and pays them for the right things, but such thinking could be more wishful than accurate.

Back to AssuraMed for an example. When Michael Petras became CEO, he was surprised to learn that the sales team was measured and compensated according to *past* sales success.

More specifically, sales reps were paid a commission on their historical "book of business," with a much smaller portion paid according to new accounts and outbound phone call activity. The result was that a few reps spent the vast majority of their time managing large existing accounts, a setup that garnered them large commissions but did very little for the company's growth prospects.

Talk about out of whack.

Soon thereafter, Michael changed the team's compensation to be based on sales growth dollars, margin growth dollars, and customer count.

Some of the reps weren't exactly thrilled. Can you blame them? For years, they'd managed a few large, existing accounts and pulled in the bulk of the available commission dollars. But given the prospect of working for a faster-growing company, most of the sales reps decided to give it a go. And sure enough, AssuraMed quickly saw revenue and margin trends improve to unprecedented levels. In addition, the new plan allowed more sales reps to participate in the company's overall performance. Ultimately, without too much heartburn, both the sales reps and the company benefited enormously from the change.

Now, we fully realize that reexamining and sometimes refreshing the measurement and reward system in every function of a company every couple of years might sound onerous. We get that. As we said at the outset, this lever is a sweat-the-details-iest.

But compensation systems all too often stagnate. And when it comes to spurring fast growth in a slow-growth world, it's a winning one to pull.

THE COMPETITION . . . INSIDE

Our last lever allows us to talk about curling again. We can't get enough of that metaphor, it seems.

Back in our first chapter, we made the point that leaders should act like the curlers who sweep the ice, clearing the way of obstacles, as their teammates push the "stone" toward the net. And by "obstacles," we said to complete the metaphor, we meant dumb bureaucratic hurdles and hoops.

The same applies to growth. Except the obstacles for a growth initiative aren't just dumb bureaucratic hurdles and hoops. No, they're also the jealous, petty resisters within the "old" organization who resent the money and attention being lavished on the new, little venture in their midst.

They hate it.

"It's all senior management talks about. It has no future," they complain. "It's soaking the place of money. We make it—they spend it."

Ah, human nature.

Now, on one level, such resisters can't really harm a new growth initiative. All they're doing is moaning and groaning, right? But on the other hand, their subterfuge can take a real toll. They can drag their feet in sharing information about customers or suppliers. They can withhold important, relevant, or useful information or ideas in meetings. They can find a thousand little ways not to cooperate and collaborate, killing the growth initiative's chances of success with a thousand little cuts.

Worst of all, they can keep their best people hidden from the new growth venture, using all sorts of excuses. "We can't spare

Mary until we get through the quarter; the customers won't have it," or, "John doesn't want to change positions this year; he's got a baby coming." This kind of behavior, the hoarding of people, is the biggest sin of growth resisters. It's 100 times harder to start something new than to run a $300 million, 50-year-old division with all its customers locked in and all its systems humming.

And so the final lever to pull, and pull hard, in order to stimulate growth, is to co-opt growth's resisters. Identify them, defuse them, and redirect them. Sometimes a pointed conversation about mission and behaviors will do. But it sure helps to bring out the heavy artillery, linking a significant portion of the old guard's bonuses to the growth initiative's success. The wallet, in this kind of circumstance, really helps focus the mind. If that doesn't work, resisters have to go. They kill growth.

Regardless of which tactic you choose, just know this: Every growth initiative faces tough competition outside your company walls. The leader's job—and we mean leaders at every level—is to make sure there's none inside as well.

How can we catalyze growth? Across every industry and geography, it's the same burning question. Everywhere we've been, everywhere we go, everyone we've talked to wants to know how to grow faster in what's become an intractably slow-growth world.

Our answer to that challenge lies in the drivers we've described above. But the truth is, on one level, this whole book is about growth. Great leadership leads to growth. Great teams lead to growth. Great strategy leads to growth. Great data crunching leads to growth. Great, refreshed compensation plans lead to growth.

You get where we're going with this.

And that's why, when we first spoke to Michael Petras at AssuraMed about his team's 30 percent increase in the company's growth rate, he told us, "We did everything all at once."

Yes, he pulled all the right levers. He brought in fresh eyes. He didn't sprinkle when it came to resource allocation; he assigned his best people to growth ventures. He measured and rewarded performance around growth goals. He made innovation everyone's job. And if anyone tried to undermine growth initiatives, he made sure they wouldn't again.

It all worked. The company continues to grow—in 2014, it surpassed $1 billion in sales—and the best part of it, for Michael and for us, is how that makes its people feel. Growth energizes everyone it touches. It's just so exciting.

Exciting—and imperative. In nature, anything that isn't growing is dying. The same is true in business. Without a doubt, these are slow-growth times globally. Sometimes it can seem like just staying even with the previous quarter or year is a victory. But growth is so vital to making work meaningful and fun, you can't let yourself believe that stasis is the status quo.

Only growth is—and it's great.

4. GLOBALIZATION: IT'S COMPLICATED

Y ou can love or hate Facebook, but you cannot argue with how clever it is for labeling one of its relationship statuses, "It's complicated." Everyone gets what that little phrase means. You're in a mess you can't live without.

Just like globalization.

Look, it would be ridiculous to write a book claiming to address the real challenges of business today and not talk about the good, bad, and ugly of getting work done in foreign markets. It would be just as ridiculous to act as if advice on getting globalization right was in short supply. Good grief, it's ubiquitous.

Lots of such advice is good. Some of it is great. And here's some good news. We're going to try not to repeat what you've already heard from both categories. Instead, we'd like to talk about the usually un-talked-about stuff. The stuff that, we believe, really makes a difference when you're doing business across borders. Our insights come from (one of us) working for 40 years in a global conglomerate and then, more recently, (both of us) working with dozens of companies of every kind and size doing business overseas. And from those experiences, we'd posit that, along with the old standbys, there are four vital elements to globalizing successfully. Perhaps your organization has already happened onto some of them. Others may strike you as new. For instance, we rarely hear people talk about the importance of discernment in globalization, and yet we view it as perhaps the most essential quality a global manager can possess. More on that later.

Familiar or not, let's get at each vital element without further ado by asking (and answering) the following four questions.

I. IS OUR GLOBALIZATION INITIATIVE A WIN-WIN?

OK, did that hurt? If so, you're not alone. For some reason, scads of companies—even good, smart companies—march into global initiatives with a "make a killing" mentality. They're going to blow open new export markets by shoving their stuff into local distribution channels, or they're going to squeeze sourcing costs down to nearly nothing. The whole idea is *cha-ching*.

But you know and we know business doesn't work that way, or at least, not for very long.

Take exporting.

True, there was a time, say about 25 years ago, when Western companies could show up in foreign markets, sign up local distribution for their products, and count on some level of success. After all, in those days, Western products had an enormous value-add. China, for example, wasn't churning out modern, highly efficient farm equipment; India wasn't producing mobile ultrasound machines.

Today, of course, China and India have their own well-trained engineers and state-of-the-art factories, and many more countries do, too. Poland, for instance, and more recently, Nigeria . . . The list of developed and developing nations with healthy, home-grown economies is growing every year. This expansion of prosperity is very good news.

But it does mean that you have to think twice before you throw money into an exporting strategy. "Do we have something truly unique," you need to ask, "that the intended market wants and needs? Is our technology exceptional and revolutionary? Can we protect it from getting easily copied and quickly sold for less?" If the answer to any of these questions is no, your distributors might win. You most likely will not.

One caveat here, and it's a big one. If your product and technology aren't unique, a strong brand can be a significant mitigating factor in creating a win-win situation. Miller's Pabst Blue Ribbon is a premium beer brand in China—go figure—selling for upwards of $30 a bottle. Nestlé's Kit Kat brand is wildly popular in Japan, sold in 80 varieties, including flavors like soybean, grilled corn, and lemon vinegar. Such examples, of course, are not limited to consumables. Nike, Apple, Chanel, and American Express are all powerhouse global brands, and have surely been able to create win-win arrangements with their many local partners.

We might add here that a lack of brands is one of China's biggest challenges in the next decade. You can count on one hand the country's "gotta have" products, right? Contrast that with Japan and Korea, which, over the past 40 and 20 years respectively, have poured billions into creating household names. Think Samsung LG and Hyundai. Who knows when China will catch up? Probably in the next decade. That said, even if it's a bit longer, it's a time frame not to be lost on exporters currently counting on their brands as cover.

Now to sourcing, which, like exporting, is not what it used to be. Forget milking your offshore operations; that's so 1985. Today, without a reasonable upside—without a true win-win—for the local producer, your arrangement will eventually blow apart.

We love a win-win sourcing example that comes from David's Bridal, the largest wedding gown retailer in the United States. For many years, according to chairman Paul Pressler, David's had sourced its intricate technical sewing from ten Chinese factories, but starting in around 2013, the company began to feel the arrangement exposed it to too much risk in terms of rising labor costs, political uncertainty, and captive logistics. And so it decided to expand its commitment to its one factory partnership in Sri Lanka, which was run by an entrepreneur who had proven successful in producing high-quality goods at very competitive prices. For its part, David's Bridal provided 25 percent of the capital, technical training, and an initial production guarantee of five years. This enabled the entrepreneur to cover early losses and secure outside capital investment. "Supply chains are a very potent weapon for us," Paul Pressler explains.

"We wanted to be important to our partner in Sri Lanka and him to be very important to us so we could work together for a long time."

"Long time" is right. Because, ultimately, the key to creating a global business win-win is a time-horizon thing.

Vindi Banga, a longtime Unilever executive (now working in private equity) and a storehouse of knowledge about globalization, tells an all-too-familiar narrative about how many joint ventures (JV) fall apart. "Everything always starts out wonderfully," he says. "Everyone is smiling and shaking hands. It all feels very equal. The big guy thinks he's bringing technology or branding, and the small guy thinks he's bringing local markets, contacts, and regulatory knowledge. It's a nice, fair deal."

Five years pass, in Vindi's account. The JV has been a success, so much so that the "big guy" wants to scale up. Sometimes it does so by buying out the local partner, who can end up feeling used, and occasionally, even angry and exploited enough to turn around and become a competitor, a less-than-optimal outcome. In other cases, the "big guy" proposes a deal. "Let's each put in another $50 million," he tells his local partner. The local partner balks—that's more than he has in the bank or could dream of obtaining with a loan. In most cultures, however, this message is embarrassing, and so the local partner pushes back with "You're ramping up too early," or "We're not making enough money for that kind of additional commitment."

The big guy becomes annoyed. "You're going to get us in trouble with that attitude," he says. "We've got competitors we need to stay ahead of."

With such back-and-forth, "They're talking right past each

other," Vindi says, "and the trouble begins." Slowly but surely, the JV starts to fall apart, and it usually implodes with the big guy finding another, "more willing" local manufacturer, that is, someone with deeper pockets. The original partner is left behind, feeling shafted.

This problem occurs too often, Vindi says, "because the partners never sat down at the beginning and thought about the five- or ten-year plan. It seems so simple, but it rarely happens."

Similarly, too many companies are shortsighted when it comes to the *length* of global assignments for their managers working abroad. The fact is, if you want a win-win, you cannot send your people for one- or two-year gigs. Your local partners will be numbed by an ever-changing cast of characters. And your people? Well, here's how Vindi Banga describes it. "The first year is useless; you don't know if you're coming or going. Everything has to be learned," he says. "You're constantly confused. You're asleep when your company at home is awake, and you're awake when they're asleep.

"By the second year, you're beginning to get the local customs and markets, and finding and entering into the relationships you need. By the third year, you're finally functioning."

That's right, *third* year. That's when many expats are starting to talk with their bosses back home about wrapping it up. They're weary. They miss their relatives. But frankly, that's when the good stuff is just beginning.

Bottom line: if your goal is a win-win situation—and globally, our point is that it needs to be—play more than fair and plan for the long term.

Think about it as buying uncomplication insurance.

2. ARE WE SENDING PEOPLE WITH THE SINGLE QUALITY THEY NEED THE MOST, DISCERNMENT?

Some clichés are clichés because they're true, including the one about putting your best, most talented people on foreign assignments. Foreign assignments may seem glamorous from afar, but up close, in the trenches, they're brutally hard, fraught with peculiarities, obstacles, and government bureaucrats. Without a doubt, it's easier to run a $500 million, 50-year-old division in the home country than a start-up in Poland or China. One hums along. The other bumps, careens, and stalls with alarming frequency.

Furthermore, everyone knows how hard it can be to fill foreign assignments—especially if, as in our previous point, the assignment should last several years. People have families and friends; they have homes and hobbies. They have a career trajectory that they aspire to, and they're afraid of being forgotten. There's a reason that old song from *Cheers* is so familiar. It's true: "Sometimes you want to go where everybody knows your name." And not just sometimes—a lot of the time.

Which is why so many companies end up sending the not-quite-right people abroad. They assign the eager, the ambitious, the adventurous, the inveterate travelers, the dual-passport holders, the MBA who happened to live in India until he was five. They send the manager from HR or operations who has two years left until retirement and wouldn't mind spending them on a sort of mini-vacation with his or her spouse. And surely some, even many, of these people will have valuable skills and abilities.

But too many lack discernment, which our experience tells us is the single most important quality expats need to be effective. Yep, discernment's the biggie.

And what's discernment? Good judgment, basically. Or more precisely in this context, it's the combination of business savvy, cultural sensitivity, and good old wisdom. It's the ability and self-confidence to know when to push forward the company's will and ways, and when not to, out of respect for local customs and mores.

Two stories from Disney demonstrate what we mean.

In the first, the company was opening its first store in Japan. The idea was to go Disney all the way—creating a big, exciting, interactive retail experience starting at the front door, with a bevy of cheery greeters.

Disney's Japanese executives adamantly opposed the plan. Japanese shoppers, they explained, were accustomed to greeters who bowed politely and kept their distance. Any other approach wouldn't just be awkward, they asserted, it would be rude.

Disney's local leader on the ground heard the message, but decided to go forward with greeters anyway. Engagement, friendliness, "high touch"—they were all part of Disney's brand DNA. Japanese customers might not like the greeters at first, they said, but they would grow to love them. And indeed they did. Within two years, Disney's store in Tokyo was among its most profitable in the world. (It should be noted, many "indigenous" Tokyo department stores now have greeters.)

By contrast, before Disney even opened its theme park in Hong Kong, it decided to bend to an important local custom. At issue, according to Paul Pressler, who worked at Disney for 15 years before taking charge of David's Bridal and is the source of both these anecdotes, was something critical. Seating in every restaurant on the property.

At Disney parks around the world, restaurants offer tables of varying sizes and seating times that span several hours. "What we learned during the market research phase of the Hong Kong project was that it was part of the culture for people to eat all at the same time, basically at noon, and seated all at one table or in very large groups," Paul recalls.

Again, a debate and a decision. How people took their meals was not critical to Disney's DNA, and trying to change that custom wasn't going to make anyone's Disney experience better. Thus, the dining rooms would be designed and staffed to accommodate a large-table noon seating. The local practice took precedence.

Again, success. That's what discernment leads to. It's a subtle thing, we get that. But you'll know it when you see it, playing out in decisions large and small, showing itself as good judgment and self-confidence. That's the double helix of traits you need to take on headquarters when needed, or to work through prickly, and often significant, differences with local managers. And when you see such discernment in action, grab those individuals. They're the ones who will give your foreign operations the best chance to thrive. They can make all the difference in the world.

3. ARE WE BEING REAL ABOUT RISK?

It goes without saying (well, practically, since we're saying it) that global ventures invite a whole new level of risk into your business. The first and most obvious way to deal with that reality, of course, is to limit your dependence on one country, particularly when it comes to sourcing. That's the main reason, incidentally, that David's Bridal decided to open a factory in Sri Lanka. As satisfied as the company was (and is) with its Chinese partners, "we just felt too much exposure," as Paul Pressler puts it.

The second way to manage global risk is also pretty obvious: go overboard with compliance. It doesn't make any difference what the rules are in the country where you're doing business, if employees are permitted to work seven days a week, or factories can be built without foundations, and all the like. You must adhere to the compliance rules of your home country, which will invariably be stricter, safer, and more protective of workers and the environment. You must obsessively think "global best practice" in all of your processes. Will this all be more expensive? Of course it will. It doesn't matter, because should an accident occur, the human and financial cost of your cutting corners will prove far more so.

You know the tragic stories that make our point here. There are too many of them. Take heed.

Speaking of compliance, there may come a time when someone utters the phrase "facilitating gratuity" or "facilitating payments" to you. Hello, that's how bribery starts. You will likely feel stunned, and you should. Sure, some locals may tell you, "Don't worry, that's how it's done here." A few of your own colleagues may even look away, worn out by years of pressure to keep up with competitors. Regardless, hold firm. Walk away. Cover your ears—whatever—just don't capitulate. Yes, in the short run, you may lose business to other companies that "play ball." But in the long term, you will be rewarded by becoming the gold standard of integrity. And your risk profile (not to mention your conscience) will be all the better for it.

To quote Vindi Banga on this point, "It takes just one mistake to destroy decades of a carefully built reputation based on ethical practice." Leaders must be ruthless when ferreting out and punishing offenders. He adds, "More importantly, they must be seen to be ruthless." There's no point penalizing bribery in private.

Finally, when it comes to managing global risk, perhaps the one story that doesn't get told enough is about the importance of sweating the gritty, grimy details.

Really sweating them. Because you cannot delegate your overseas activities to a middleman, especially in the early stages. Many trading companies and consultants and all the like will beckon—"We know the local people and customs and regulations," they will tell you, "let us facilitate your expansion . . ." In fact, some of these firms and individuals can be useful. But you need to be in the room with them while they do their work. In fact, you need to be elbow-to-elbow.

Consider, as an example, Bunny Williams, the renowned interior decorator who, after four decades as a solo practitioner, decided to launch a branded furniture business in 2010, with a wide array of pieces manufactured overseas. Talk about a true entrepreneur—a brand-new business idea based on globalization! Indeed, globalization is hardly limited to corporations. Many small businesses operate abroad, and some, like Bunny Williams Home, as her furniture business is called, offer great examples of best practices at work.

Today, with the business thriving, Bunny offers the following piquant advice. "You cannot go global on the phone or online," she says. "You have to go there, get into the factories, build the relationships, talk to the craftsmen, stand there and watch them work, watch them pack and crate your stuff, talk to them about logistics. No one else can do it better than you can because no one cares as much."

As Bunny set up her business, she spent six weeks over the course of every year visiting her manufacturers in China and Vietnam. To further manage her risk around quality and delivery, she started with very small orders at each facility, 100 pieces at a time.

"I'm small. I can't come in and make all sorts of demands. But I can do my homework and get into every little detail," Bunny explains. "That takes time. It has to."

Importantly, such time investment cannot ebb when the venture gets up and running. To this day, Bunny visits her factories at least twice a year, spending days with their managers and (using a translator) speaking with the craftsmen doing the work. "It can be exhausting," she admits, "and very hot."

But being real about risk is like that. Along with the big, obvious things, like diversifying your locations and overdoing it on compliance, you have to sweat the small stuff, sometimes even literally.

4. ARE WE TAKING FULL ADVANTAGE OF OUR FOREIGN FORAY'S UPSIDE?

If you knew someone who visited New York to see the Statue of Liberty, you'd think they were nuts to go right home without taking in a show on Broadway, right? And yet that's how too many companies think about their foreign activities. They're in India to have a call center, say, or in Indonesia to manufacture shoes, full stop.

That's wearing blinders. Going global is expensive and risky; it can take years to become profitable. But more often than most companies realize, you can hasten the profitability of a global initiative by expanding into markets nearby, as long as it is, as we said earlier, a win-win. When David's Bridal started sourcing in China, for instance, its goal was to lower prices and shorten delivery time for brides back in America. It soon realized, however, that its Chinese operations created the economics to open new export markets in Japan and Brazil. Indeed, more and more companies are using their offshore operations as headquarters to sell their sourced products globally.

Another way to take full advantage of your global activities is by capitalizing on what they offer in terms of innovation.

Yes, innovation. Every foreign market you operate in is a laboratory for it. Bunny Williams, as an example, was visiting her Vietnam factory when she noticed craftsmen applying a lacquer finish to a local product. "It was so beautiful, I went home and designed a whole new line of lacquer furniture for them to build," she relates. "It's been a huge hit." Similarly, when Unilever first started selling shampoo in Asia, it quickly realized that most consumers did not have the money to buy a bottle at a time. The company responded by creating one-wash shampoo packets, which it could sell for pennies. Unilever could have left it at that, but the idea clearly had potential in other markets, and was soon rolled out around the world, to phenomenal success.

Bottom line: Global markets aren't just for exporting or sourcing. They're for learning and innovating.

To miss that opportunity is to miss half the fun (and value) of going global.

As we said at the outset, we know there's a world of advice out there on going global. Pundits opine. Professors pronounce. Veterans of the foreign markets have their war stories. None of this counsel, ours included, will probably ever make globalization less complicated. How could it? Business at home is complicated enough.

But we do think that the four questions posed here get at the real-world part of making globalization successful. Make every partnership a win-win. Only send your people oozing with discernment. Get sweaty about risk. And stop thinking about your offshore operations as offshore operations. They're outposts for expansion and innovation.

Then, after all that, get excited. Done right, globalization can be terrifically rewarding for a company's bottom line and its collective brain.

And that's a pretty uncomplicated thing to love.

5. FEAR OF FINANCE . . . NO MORE

If you work on Wall Street, or pass your days in the conference rooms and cubicles of corporate finance, or somewhere along the way picked up a degree in accounting and a CFA, this chapter is not for you.

This chapter is for the people in business who consider finance with fear and perhaps even loathing.

Hello, you are legion. And not just among business newcomers, either. From what we've heard time and again, finance strikes some degree of panic into the hearts of more than a few been-around-the-block-ers, too.

By finance, to be clear, we're not talking about the raw basics. Revenues, expenses, net income—that stuff is plain enough and most everyone gets it walking in the door. Moreover, most people with more than a year or two in business understand which numbers drive their unit's or division's performance. For manufacturing people, it could be inventory turns and unit cost. For marketing people, it could be new account closings, customer retention, and sales growth. For call center managers, it could be the time it takes to answer, number of dropped calls, and employee retention.

No, when we talk about fear of finance, we mean you feel vaguely queasy before presenting your budget to the powers-that-be. Or you worry you're just not good enough at math to ever *really* understand what all those figures on the PowerPoint slides mean. Or you get lost in meetings with CFO types when the acronyms start flying, and boy, can they fly. DCRR, EBIT, EBITDA, yadda yadda yadda.

Basically, to you, finance sounds like a language spoken in a country where you've never lived.

Our goal in this chapter is to fix that "problem." Not that we're promising instant expertise—not by any means. Finance, like any function in business, is a nuanced body of knowledge that can take years to master. But listen, you don't have to be fluent in French to have a great time in Paris. You just need to know the terms that are essential for getting around, and the landmarks that will make your visit meaningful. Put together, such knowledge can transform you from a clueless tourist to an informed visitor.

The same goes for finance. There are terms with which you definitely need to be familiar: cash flow for starters, plus the components of the balance sheet, and the components of the operating statement. But most of all, you need a mental map—a mindset, if you will—that says, "When it comes to finance, I have one main interest, and it's variance analysis."

Oh, how we love variance analysis—comparing key numbers month over month, or year over year, or comparing them to plan, to see what's working in your organization and what isn't. We love variance analysis when you're considering an acquisition, using it to test the assumptions beneath the forecasts. We love it during long-range planning sessions, when variance analysis is the driving force behind questions like, "What makes you think that our competitors will stay static while we gain share?" And we hope that by the end of this chapter you'll come to love variance analysis, too. Because variance analysis is the *aha* part of finance. The part that spurs you to peer inside the numbers, pick them apart, debate their significance, and assess the doors they open and close. It's the part of finance that impels you to understand "the numbers" for what they are: a means to making better business decisions.

Variance analysis is, to bring back a leadership imperative from Chapter 1, the *truth-seeking* part of finance. It's the discussion that, more than any other, uncovers the real world in all its possibility, risk, and complexity. It's a spotlight and a microscope at once, a super-tool so useful the only thing you should be scared of is what you miss if you don't use it.

HOW HEALTHY ARE WE?

Before we turn to the components of financial statements and variance analysis, a short, related detour.

More than occasionally, people ask us, "As a manager, what

number should I care about the most?" Or put another way, "Which financial ratio gives me the best read on my organization's overall health?" Sometimes this question is followed by presumed answers. "Is it return on investment (ROI) or return on sales (ROS)?" we hear. "Is it the quick ratio?" And so on.

Ah, if only a business's well-being could be boiled down to one figure.

It can't, needless to say, but if you're running a business, whether it's a corner store or a multi-product multinational, we would say there are three key indicators that are very helpful: employee engagement and customer satisfaction—both of which are not technically financial—and cash flow, which is.

Employee engagement first. It goes without saying that no company, small or large, can win over the long run without energized employees who believe in the mission and understand how to achieve it. That's why a company needs to take measure of employee engagement at least once a year through anonymous surveys in which people feel completely safe to speak their minds.

Just be careful. If you can influence it, don't let your company fall into the common trap of letting these surveys devolve into questionnaires about the little stuff, such as the tastiness of the food in the company cafeteria or the availability of spaces in the parking lot. The most meaningful surveys probe how employees feel about the strategic direction of the company and the quality of their career opportunities. They ask questions such as these: Do you feel the company cares about you and that you have been given the opportunity to grow? Do you feel that your everyday work is connected to what company leaders say in speeches and in the annual report? Basically, the best employee surveys get at one question: just how aligned are we?

As we noted in Chapter 3, growth is the key to any company's long-term viability, which is why customer satisfaction is the second vital sign. This metric, we believe, is optimally assessed via site visits, and not just with your "good" customers. Managers need to go see the customers whose orders are inconsistent or dropping—the ones the salespeople don't like to see themselves. And make these visits about learning. Find a dozen ways to ask: "What can we do better?"

Along with visits, we also recommend utilizing Net Promoter Score, the customer satisfaction measurement system invented by consultant Fred Reichheld. NPS centers on the question, "How likely is it that you would recommend our company, product, or service to a friend or colleague?" Customer favorites Amazon and Apple are reported to have NPS scores of around 70 out of a possible 100, while the near-monopolistic cable TV industry as a whole is said to be closer to 30.

While NPS is a great way to get unvarnished customer feedback, we've found it also has a terrific secondary benefit. We use NPS every quarter to measure the satisfaction of students in our MBA program. Its "report card" aspect provides a road map of rich qualitative comments that really gets our team fired up, and happily, gives them reason to celebrate, too. NPS, it turns out, measures customer satisfaction, but at the same time, when leaders use it to quickly address customer concerns, it also elevates employee engagement. It does double duty.

Finally, when you talk about taking a company's pulse, there's cash flow, which, as we've said, also happens to be one of the must-know terms if you're ever to get comfortable with finance.

Here's some good news. Cash is not complicated.

Every company tracks cash flow three ways. Cash flow from operating activities is the money that flows out of regular business operations, basically revenues less every last expense. Cash flow from investing activities mainly reflects major assets that a company bought or sold, as well as the gains or losses it achieved in the financial markets. Cash flow from financing activities represents the net of new equity, cash dividends, and changes in the company's debt position.

The main thing to know about cash flow is that it just does not lie. It tells you in raw, hard numbers how much money went out, how much came in, and how much you have. That's why so many managers and investors like it more than net income as a measure of profitability. Net income comes out of the P&L statement, which is embedded with assumptions and judgments. Free cash flow, on the other hand, gives you a sense of your company's maneuverability—whether you can return cash to shareholders, pay down debt, borrow more to grow faster, or any combination of these options. Cash flow helps you understand and control your destiny.

Now, without a doubt there are lots of ways to measure the pulse of a business. We like these three because they're directionally correct. They'll give you a good feel for the health of your business.

But they're not enough. They're not enough to hold your own in a meeting where numbers are the main event, the kind of meeting where you've been called upon, say, to present your budget or a proposed investment to your boss or the board, or even to colleagues. They're not enough to hold your own in a meeting that you've called yourself, either, the kind where you're being presented to, and you need to evaluate a budget or an investment.

Because that's where so much of finance happens—in meetings, right? Around tables, where everyone is staring at reams of charts, calculations, and pro formas, and PowerPoint slides keep rolling by like floats in the Macy's Thanksgiving Day Parade.

For those sessions, you can't just be a spectator. You need to get in the mix, and you can.

IT ALL BALANCES OUT

Every company has a balance sheet, but unless you work at a small organization or start-up where cash is the whole ball game, you could go your whole career without ever thinking much about it. That's understandable, as the balance sheet is mainly of interest to those people in the company concerned with the organization's financial position, who are thinking about borrowing money from the markets, or approving investments, say, to build a new plant or start a new business. If your company is public, the balance sheet is also of interest to financial analysts and investors, who are wondering, among other things, "Hmm, is this company liquid enough to do everything it claims it's going to be doing?"

In short—very short—the balance sheet summarizes a company's assets, liabilities, and its shareholder's equity, and in doing so, gives a picture of what a company owns and owes, as well as the amount invested in it by individuals and the markets. It's called a balance sheet because, well, it balances out. On the left side, you have the company's assets. On the right, you have its liabilities and shareholders' equity.

Assets can be all sorts of things, depending on the type of business. The usual suspects, though, are cash, accounts receivable, raw materials, buildings, factories, inventory, and property. Some assets are said to be "intangible," because you generally can't see, touch, or sit on them; but they happen to be very important for some companies, namely goodwill, patents, licenses, and copyrights.

Liabilities? In layman's terms, they're debts; they're what the company owes to outside parties, both short- and long-term. Shareholder equity is the money invested in the company by the company's owner or owners, the markets, or both.

We're done.

Really, we are. Just know that the balance sheet is a picture of a company's financial "flexibility" at a given moment in time. For the purposes of the people reading this chapter—that is, finance's fear-and-loathing crowd—that's the most important thing you need to know about it.

And probably, unless you have a secret desire to become your company's next CFO, the only thing.

WELCOME TO THE SAUSAGE FACTORY

The income statement is another matter entirely. Instead of depicting liquidity, it depicts profitability. Or to be a little bit more specific about it, it reports how much is being sold, how much those sales are costing to create, and what's left over when all is said and done.

The income statement is a visit to the sausage factory.

And you know what? No one in business can really escape it. Sure, you can hold an entry-level or individual contributor-type position at some companies, and the income statement won't impact (or intrude on) your day-to-day activities. But you can be sure of two things: the income statement impacts your boss's life, and someday, if your career progresses, it will inevitably impact yours.

Take the case of a woman we'll call Mary here. For several years, Mary worked at a large consumer products company as a fragrance designer—she held a master's in chemistry and also had an MBA. After successfully leading a few teams and showing real verve in suggesting advertising concepts for new perfumes, she was promoted to general manager of a different fragrance division in the mass-market space.

Before Mary was promoted—she was replacing an executive who'd been let go—Mary had all sorts of ideas about change, even from a distance. Introducing a fragrance for pregnant moms, for instance, was one of her favorites. She also had strong opinions about which fragrance designers in her new division needed to go because their noses were "outdated," and had her eye on an outside perfume consultant that she thought should be hired.

Ah yes, that was before Mary's first meeting with her new, inherited team to discuss the division's annual budget and long-range plan.

That was, you might say, before Mary's heart attack.

Not a real one, of course, but the kind you have as a manager when you look at the numbers, as Mary did that first day of P&L responsibility, and see your unit's marketing costs going up 5 percent a year for the previous three years, while revenues were flat over the same period. The kicker was that her predecessor's forecast was for more of the same for the next three years.

"Well, now I see why he's gone," Mary thought that day. "But what did I just get myself into?"

She got herself, as all managers do, into the middle of a story. That's right—the income statement tells a story. Sometimes it's very scary. Sometimes it's just a bit worrisome. Other times, the story is reason to break out the champagne and start planning grand things. Regardless, the income statement tells you a lot. About the trade-offs the business has been making, and about how the business is doing.

It's a story about the past and present, and, more important, it's an invitation to a conversation about the future.

A great, big, exciting, truth-seeking conversation.

IT'S ALL RELATIVE

If there is just one concept you take from this chapter, please let it be the following: numbers are not just meant to be calculated. Numbers are mainly meant to be compared. And inasmuch, they're meant to start conversations about *variance*.

Now, what exactly is variance?

It can be the gap between the results that were expected in the "plan," and the results that were delivered in real life, as in, "What's going on? Our raw-material costs ran away from us last quarter."

It can be the gap between results delivered in the past and results projected for the future, as in, "Wow, they're projecting sales of good old Product X are going to shoot up like a hockey stick two years out. What makes you think that's going to happen?"

Variance can be virtually any change you see on a financial statement—up or down—that makes you perplexed, uneasy, or curious enough to ask, "Why?"

Now, every manager has certain favorite financial figures or ratios that he or she likes to keep an eye on for variances. And that makes sense. With time and experience in any given business or industry, you come to discover which trends are the most reliable harbingers of good news or early warning signs of bad. Of course, how often you check on your "favorite" variances is related to the nature of the business—short cycle or long, tech, industrial, or service. The top teams at McDonald's and Burger King certainly look at receipts on a daily basis. While at most long-cycle businesses, say, like those making power plant turbines or jet planes, managers normally scrutinize variances on a monthly or quarterly basis.

All that being said, and mainly for the purpose of giving you options to consider, we thought we'd mention several variances that, in our experience and estimation, have really proven their worth over the decades.

Sales and net income are always important numbers to track, but the truth is, by the time you see them for many businesses, they're telling a story about the past and can have somewhat limited utility in telling the future. Orders and salaried employment, by contrast, have an uncanny way of serving as proxies for future sales and costs. A significant increase in the order rate is good news,

THE REAL-LIFE MBA

but almost certain to signal that production output and overall costs are going to need adjusting. Meanwhile, salaried employment by function—which can be looked at monthly, quarterly, or annually—is a good way to see what part of the organization is hiring, so that you can figure out why. Is there a new program, or, perhaps, is someone busy empire-building? At the very least, this figure is a good harbinger of changes in the cost structure.

Quarterly variances in the operating margin rate and working capital turnover ratio are great indicators, we would suggest, of how an organization's efficiency is trending. Obviously, you want these numbers to be high and improving steadily.

Longer term, we like keeping close track of return on investment (ROI) and market share. Increasing the former makes investors happy, as well it should, and the latter reflects customer satisfaction, another measurement we commended previously.

Again, we mention these figures because they've been useful in our experience. The bigger point, however, is that, if you're a nonfinance person "doing" finance, variance analysis is where you need to dwell. Whether you're in a small, informal meeting looking at an investment. Whether you're in a formal budget review. Whether you're attending an anything-goes long-range planning session.

Always, always focus on the variances. Use them to ferret out the truth of people's assumptions, hopes, fears, and agendas.

PUSH AND PROBE

Let's return to Mary, the perfume business GM, for a minute. As you might recall, Mary's first encounter with her division's financials delivered an alarming story of marketing costs steadily rising and revenues holding flat.

Her reaction was perfect. With her team around her, and their conference room blocked off for the entire day, she dug in. In a very technical phrase, that's the activity of variance analysis, too: digging in. You take the numbers one at a time, pull them apart, question where they came from and why, debate where they're going and how that can happen, and generally just push, push, push, and probe, probe, probe.

In Mary's case, not surprisingly, the conversation quickly turned to the division's escalating marketing costs, and it didn't take long for the people around the table to throw in their old boss as the culprit, and more specifically, his pet social media project.

"It was supposed to pay for itself in eighteen months," the CFO reported sardonically. "We're still waiting."

"Well, who owns that project now?" Mary pushed back. "It's still in the budget. Who's running it and measuring its effectiveness?"

The answer, it turned out, was no one. Mary immediately assembled a SWAT team, including some people in the room, to determine if the social media campaign should live, die, or be otherwise modified.

But more important, the revelation that the division's social media campaign was essentially an orphan prompted a rigorous, hours-long debate around the table about the marketing budget and strategic direction overall. If the social media project was killed, Mary asked, where should the freed-up dollars go? Should they be diverted back to more traditional magazine advertising, or redeployed to R&D to create new products?

"How about neither?" came one reply. "Our whole space is about celebrity fragrances. Either we buy big names or we die."

Let's just say not everyone agreed with that assertion, but Mary made sure everyone's voice was heard. Again, that's an inherent part of the variance analysis, seeking the truth from every point of view.

Mary and her team also dug into why selling, general, and administrative (SG&A) expenses were trending upward. "Do we really need eight people in HR?" she asked the department's leader. At first, unaccustomed to such candor, he shot back an offended, "Excuse me?" But the back-and-forth that followed opened up a productive conversation about HR's role in finding, developing, and retaining top talent, how some felt it wasn't doing that, and whether the department might be able to do a better job with half the staff but better talent.

Last but not least, the variance analysis that day led to a spirited debate about untapped sources of revenue. "Looking back, you can see our best growth was three to four percent year over year," Mary said to her team. "That has to be our target for next year, and as we look forward, I'm asking you to come up with some bold ideas to double that growth rate three years out. At our next meeting, let's discuss what we need to do next year to make that happen, and identify the roadblocks that might make that challenge unreasonable."

Now, such conversations are often contentious. And the rigorous debate they generate can be uncomfortable. That's OK. Actually, that's more than OK. Truth-seeking is rarely a day by the pool with a piña colada.

Perhaps that's exactly why variance analysis makes business

better and smarter. It keeps it aligned. Is that process messy? It sure can be.

And if it's not, feel free to go ahead and make it that way.

Here's the bottom line.

You don't need to be a math whiz—you don't even really need to know all that much about the numbers—to "do" finance. You mainly need to be curious—relentlessly curious about the variances that tell you how the business is doing, where it's going, why, and how fast.

Finance isn't about keeping up with the technocrats as they throw acronyms around the room. It's about being able to use the numbers to get at the truth.

Because the truth will set you free . . . to make good business decisions.

Decisions based on sound assumptions, decisions that have examined all the options, decisions that have looked under the hood.

No matter what you do in your organization, be it in frontline sales, manufacturing, or HR, making good business decisions is your job.

To that end, the numbers are nothing to fear.

And with variance analysis, they can even be your friends.

6. WHAT TO MAKE OF MARKETING

The exact year doesn't really matter, but let's just say it was a couple of decades back that one of us attended business school, and there, on the very first day, the very first class was marketing, and the case to be cracked involved cotton-blend Fieldcrest blankets.

Here's the thing. Cotton-blend Fieldcrest blankets haven't changed much since then.

Marketing has. Has it ever.

We're speaking, in particular, about consumer marketing. It's become vastly more digital. More global. More social. More mobile. Experiential. Hypertargeted. Native. Human. Oh, we could go on and on.

Thanks to an unrelenting torrent of technology advancements

and breakthroughs in the study of consumer behavior, the brave new world of marketing just keeps getting braver and newer every day. Which is why this chapter isn't just about marketing's frontiers; it's about its fundamentals. Our goal is not to turn you into a marketing authority. Only time and experience (and probably a few mistakes along the way) will do that. But with this chapter, we hope to give you the perspective to ask the right marketing questions, no matter your role in the organization or what type of business you're in. Our goal is to give you a seat—and a voice—at the marketing table.

Look, we know that, like finance, marketing today can sometimes seem overwhelming and mysterious, filled with terminology and acronyms flung around by the burgeoning army of digital "gurus" who now seem to run the show. Surely you've heard them ballyhoo their "cutting-edge," "data-driven" insights and promises. In our experience, some of these self-anointed experts are very smart; they know something important. But many of them also make marketing today feel like an exotic bazaar, where every stall has another fortune-teller or snake-handler trying to sell you a magical ROI solution.

Right alongside marketing's technology revolution, there's the changing consumer, too. More sophisticated than ever before. Shorter attention span. Ever more immune to marketing messages. Case in point: eye-tracking research shows that many consumers have developed "ad blindness"—while perusing websites, they won't even *look* at areas of the page where they think advertisements or promotions might appear. Similarly, research strongly indicates that consumers trust recommendations from their peers on social media and review sites far more than anything they can readily identify as company-spawned marketing content.

No wonder marketing keeps reinventing itself. It has to.

But our message is this. You can't let the cacophony surrounding marketing's incessant upheaval distract you from what marketing is all about at its heart: the right product, in the right place, at the right price, with the right message, delivered by the right team.

Same as it ever was.

MUCH TRIED . . . AND STILL TRUE

Normally, we like to stay away from academic rubrics—they're just too, well, academic.

We're making an exception this time. The "Five Ps" framework, originally developed by a University of Michigan professor named E. Jerome McCarthy in 1960, remains a very useful, applicable way to explore consumer marketing, which is probably why so many MBA programs have stuck with it, including our own. (As an aside, McCarthy's framework originally only had four Ps, and was expanded to five by other academics in later decades. Also, later in this chapter, we will depart from consumer marketing's Five Ps to talk about the principles involved in the related but separate topic of business-to-business marketing.)

In a thumbnail, the Five Ps framework states that effective consumer marketing is a matter of making the right choices about your *product*, its *place* (distribution channels), its *price*, its *promotional* messaging, and finally, its *people*, that is, its organizational support.

Now, given all the changes in technology and consumer behavior we've just mentioned, it's not surprising that the conversation around many of the five Ps has significantly changed since McCarthy's day.

The first P, product, is not one of them.

Because a great product has always been, and will probably always be, the ultimate marketing play. Even with the advent of big data, social media, SEO, and price transparency. Even with Oscar-worthy beer commercials during the Super Bowl. The fact remains that marketing's killer app is a desirable product that makes the customer's life better in some way. That's just always going to be the case. Sure, a company can promote the living daylights out of a product that falls short of that standard, but such an effort is going to be expensive and, in time, unsustainable.

You cannot market meh forever.

You can only create "me-want." That is why, no matter what type of business you're in, the best marketing always starts in R&D or its equivalent. It starts with the continual improvement of current products, or the invention of irresistible and exciting new ones, with features and benefits that really matter.

That was true in 1960. It's true today. And it will be true in 2060.

Indeed, when it comes to the first P, the only truly new thing companies need to think about is that the marketplace is much more vast and crowded than it's ever been. Fieldcrest blankets used to have three competitors—all of them American manufacturers. Today, Fieldcrest has hundreds of competitors, many global, selling their wares via a vast array of platforms, both online and off.

The proliferation of products and channels has one main implication for consumer marketing, and it has to do with the cost of breaking through the clutter, a process otherwise known as "push." Increased competition makes push harder and more costly, and that's why pull, drawing customers to you by dint of your product's features, benefits, and brand story, is so critical now.

So if you ever find yourself in a meeting—and this happens a lot—where people are fighting about the minutiae of marketing plans and debating the advantages of myriad approaches, don't forget the value in going up to 10,000 feet, and asking what really matters:

Are we selling meh or me-want?

Are we plying good or great?

Are we pushing so hard because we've got no pull?

If the answer to any of these queries is worrisome, you can still go ahead and launch your marketing program. But be assured that you and your team will soon be back at the beginning, talking about the P that comes first—because it has to.

LOCATION, LOCATION, LOCATION

Not long ago, one of our children moved to Los Angeles for work, and the thought dawned on us (OK, it dawned on one of us) that her new apartment might benefit from the purchase of a rug as a housewarming gift. So, during our next visit, when she went off to work, we went off shopping.

Easy, right? Oh so wrong. There are, it turns out, roughly

30 places to purchase a cute, relatively inexpensive rug near her apartment house in LA, and about 300 places to buy the same thing online. Overwhelmed with options, we almost gave up. That is, until we found a store about five miles from her apartment that said it would match any price for a comparable rug sold online. It did, and we bought. But right before we left, we asked the salesman, "How do you make money doing this?" He sighed and said, "Sometimes we don't."

We suggest you remember this story—and all the ones you know just like it because you've lived them—when the conversation in your organization turns to distribution channel selection, that is, marketing's second P, place. There are exceptions, of course, as when Apple releases a new phone, or a hot new restaurant opens, or a new Lord of the Rings movie is released; in such cases, yes, consumers will wait for hours and pay whatever it takes, no questions asked. But generally speaking, consumers have come to develop very high expectations. They want exactly what they want, when they want it, which usually means quickly, and they want it for as little money as possible.

Announcement: that doesn't mean you need to meet those expectations.

You only need to meet them if there's value in it for your organization.

It sounds so obvious, doesn't it? And yet, in the heat of battle, as you watch your competitors jam their products through every distribution channel known to humankind, it's all too easy to start thinking you have to be everywhere, too, just to stay alive.

And, indeed, sometimes you do. Sometimes you do have to

sell your product at cost, or even at a loss, to maintain brand awareness or keep an important distributor happy. But in our experience, such instances are rare. More often, they come into being only because the people in marketing are more persuasive or have more organizational power than the people in finance.

Our point on this is pretty blunt. When it comes to place, the question to ask is not, "How many channels can we get into to reach the most eyeballs and wallets?" Rather, it should be, "Which channels should we select in order to profitably sell the most volume?"

Period.

Yes, accessibility matters. You will hear that argument time and again in your company and over your career, and, occasionally, you will make it yourself.

But when it comes to place, never let the debate in your organization get so hot that it strays from the cool, calm, perennial truth of the matter. Profitability matters too.

DOLLARS AND SENSE

And now, to the third, and probably the most straightforward marketing P, price.

Not that there's a no-fail formula for pricing your product or service correctly. There's not. In fact, as you probably know from sitting in interminable meetings, there's rarely consensus in an organization around exactly how price-sensitive consumers really are toward certain products. Such conversations can get downright contentious.

That's OK. Grappling over pricing can be very useful in surfacing critical strategic issues. What kind of customer do we want? Are we making too much of a me-too product? Is our market defined too narrowly?

But ultimately, after the strategic conversation is exhausted, there's really only one question to ask these days when it comes to pricing:

"Why don't we run a test?"

The era of guessing about pricing is just so dead. Technology killed it. Price testing is easy. It's fast. It's usually cheap. And it gives you new, powerful flexibility.

Take the example of the RealReal, an online consignment marketplace for women's luxury clothing and jewelry. (We are modest investors.) The RealReal does many things well, but near the top of the list is its relentless use of customer tracking data to dynamically adjust pricing according to supply and demand. For instance, if a dress is posted for sale for $360 at 11 a.m. on Tuesday, and it has 700 views by 1 p.m. without being purchased, its price is lowered by, say, 8 percent. There are different algorithms for every kind of product, day of the week, and time of day, and those algorithms themselves are constantly being tweaked to reflect the learning of previous tests.

These figures are purely hypothetical. But our point is not. Pricing today is about identifying the price you want to charge, a function, of course, of cost and branding, identifying the price you think your customers want and expect to pay, and then testing every point between them.

In a way, that's what companies have always done. Only

today, you can do it a lot more quickly and productively. You can do it better.

IT'S SHOWTIME

If you've ever found yourself tearing up at a commercial—and come on, who hasn't?—you know the power of marketing's fourth P, promotion, more colloquially known as messaging.

And if you've ever been in the room when people are trying to come up with messaging, you know how hard it is, especially today, with consumers who are both anesthetized by wall-to-wall marketing noise and defensive about being emotionally manipulated.

Yet, to grow, every company has to sell its stuff. How do you break through the wall?

We'd suggest two approaches. You can help implement them yourself if marketing is part of your job, or you can be the person in your organization who asks whether these approaches are being used by your own marketing team or the agency hired to help them. Either way, you'll be adding value to one of the most important things a company ever has to do.

Tell its story.

We call the first approach "experimentation without attachment."

Because successful promotion is not just about "the creative" anymore. As with pricing, it's about *testing* the creative.

We know the marketing manager at a company that designs online training products for the HR industry. This manager, let's call him John, works with a digital agency to routinely test different taglines and selling propositions for his products, running them on different websites, with different layouts and images, to different market segments. Occasionally John gets really excited about a particular piece of creative; not long ago, for instance, he fell in love with an ad that the agency came up with that proclaimed, "Turn HR into Your Competitive Advantage!" At the same time, he was particularly turned off by another one of their proposals, an ad that showed a generic-looking young man making a thumbs-up sign with the bland-sounding tagline, "Make HR Training Easy."

Over the next several weeks, the agency ran the two ads on different sites, at different times, in different sizes—you name the combination, they tried it. Simultaneously, they tested an ad the company had used two years ago that offered a volume discount on purchases made before the end of the year.

The results were clear. Regardless of channel or time period, the thumbs-up ad was the clear winner, generating the most leads and sales. Second most successful was the volume discount ad. (John had found this ad particularly "ugly" and "off-brand," by the way.) As for the "competitive advantage" ad? You guessed it, dead last.

John was only briefly peeved. He understood the reality of the situation. Getting the best creative today is all about letting go of your ego and learning to love the data, or at the very least, learning to rely on it. In the old days, there were focus groups. They delivered useful information. And sometimes they still do. But digital testing today makes focus groups seem practically antique.

Does that mean the "creative genius" model of marketing is antique, too? Of course not. Someone has to come up with the ideas to be tested in the first place. And the facts are, there will always be magic in the making of great messaging. Great messaging still and always will reach out and touch a nerve of emotional truth with the consumer. But at the end of the day, that messaging is only great if it gets results. And that's what testing tells you.

So push your organization to experiment without attachment. The results will take it from there.

The second approach we recommend when it comes to messaging is related to the first: it's experimentation with surprise.

Here's what we mean. As noted, most consumers have their backs up and their hands over their ears. You can try to reach them with a jackhammer or megaphone. Sometimes that works—otherwise there wouldn't be mattress and car dealership ads screaming at you on late-night TV.

But there's another option, which is reaching people in ways they don't expect and, in the best-case scenario, might even like.

That requires innovation.

It's funny. People sometimes think that innovation belongs to R&D, where tech geniuses invent ever more advanced devices, software, and functionality.

But marketing is innovation territory, too; in fact, it's where innovation belongs just as much as in R&D. Innovation in what you say, innovation in how and where you say it.

That's promotion's big, open frontier, and it's where you have to live.

Take what's happening with experiential marketing, the

creation of customer "experiences" as a means of increasing exposure, shareability, brand equity, and of course, sales.

Experiential marketing is not new, of course; the first articles and books about it started appearing in 1998. But in recent years, it's become a veritable wellspring of marketing innovation. Red Bull, the energy drink company, is an absolute master at the practice, linking its brand to extreme sports events in the most imaginative and exhilarating ways possible. In 2012, for instance, the company elevated their marketing plays to a whole new dimension when they funded the "Stratos Mission to transcend human limits," enabling the whole world to gather together in front of their screens to watch Felix Baumgartner jump out of a spaceship 128,000 feet above earth to break the sound barrier.

That was an experience—for Felix, obviously, but for everyone watching, too. Twitter practically exploded with excitement. It was all so new.

To our point, it was all so *surprising*.

Now, you know and we know that Red Bull funded the Stratos Mission so that someday one of us might think, "I've got a big meeting in fifteen minutes—I think I need a Red Bull!" But the thrill of what we've seen and felt through the company's engagement marketing has worn down our resistance to what was, at its core, marketing pure and simple. In fact, it pulled us in.

Promotion has to be like that now.

Neiman Marcus underwrites fashion shows at charity events. Innovation.

IBM feeds its customers a digital diet of curated content about best practices in business.

Innovation.

To promote the second season of *Suits*, USA Network dressed male models in identical outfits and dispatched them on matching bikes around New York, LA, Chicago, and San Francisco.

Innovation.

Likewise, A&E promoted its new series *Bates Motel* by installing a neon-lit vending machine dispensing free brownies "made by Norma Bates" on an Austin city street.

Freaky, yummy, memorable. And innovation pure and simple.

In every one of these cases, someone in marketing was experimenting with the end goal of surprise.

Is it easy to measure? No. Does it always work? Of course not. But neither does the same old same old. Except, apparently, when it comes to mattresses and car dealerships.

In all other cases, think experiment, think delight. Ask, "Are we doing enough with our messaging to surprise people in a good way?"

Because, when it comes to promotion, new is the new black.

NO MARKETER IS AN ISLAND

Everyone in business knows that people in different functions and divisions should talk to each other. Silos stink. We hate them and so should everyone who wants their company to thrive and grow.

We make this point to launch our discussion of the last P, the people part of marketing.

Marketing cannot be an island unto itself, no matter how tempting that feels from the inside. Because it does—that's human nature. People like to hang around with people who understand their mindsets and share the same priorities.

But insularity is death in business. It's death in marketing. That's always been true, but it's especially true now, with the increased role of technology in digital marketing, and the vital importance of doing everything quickly.

Silos kill speed. They kill ideas. They kill impact.

Take the case of a friend of ours, who works for a medical software company that relies heavily on consumer marketing. "Sally" and her team have no end of creative ideas, but few reach fruition. Why? To start, every marketing plan must undergo a week-long legal review, followed by another week going up various finance flagpoles for sign-offs. And once those two processes are complete? Another week for IT risk management assessments. And then, yet another week waiting for the Web team's "locked down" weekly deployment schedule to come around. In total, that's at least four weeks of lag time between idea and execution, making it mission impossible for even the most motivated manager to quickly launch anything new, and certainly not in time to react to something brewing on social media.

By glaring contrast, consider what happened at Oreo in 2013.

Despite being part of a multinational conglomerate, Oreo made it a priority as an organization to align its internal teams for strong cross-department agility, so the company could be poised to spontaneously capitalize on the kind of unexpected cultural moments that can crop up in an instant these days. And indeed, such an instant came during the Super Bowl that year, when the stadium lights went out accidentally during the third quarter.

Well, it just so happened—by intent—that Oreo had its CMO,

brand manager, general counsel, and all other critical stakeholders sitting in a room together watching the game. Within minutes, they were able to launch a Twitter campaign called, "You Can Still Dunk in the Dark."

The result? From a single tweet that cost exactly zero dollars in media spend, the brand generated 525 million earned media impressions—that's multiples of the number of people who actually watched the game. It made headlines in over 100 countries. It won 14 advertising awards and *Wired* magazine even declared Oreo the winner of the Super Bowl.

The Oreo story proves that the "people" part of the Five Ps framework is not just a matter of where marketing sits in the organization. Sure, it's always been right up there with finance and R&D. The bigger point is that marketing has to sit inside and beside and within every function in an organization. Even if you're not the CEO or a senior manager, you can still advocate for that arrangement, and even informally work to make it happen. All it takes is the courage and discipline to step outside your silo, and, be it with a conversation or a question, invite the rest of the organization into yours.

Because today, marketing is everybody's business.

AND THAT INCLUDES B2B

In recent years, business-to-business marketing (or B2B, as it is commonly called) has undergone just as much change as business-to-consumer (B2C) marketing, for much the same reasons. More technology. Savvier global buyers and suppliers. Increased competitiveness. Heightened transparency.

Again, our goal is not to make you a functional expert. It's to put you at the B2B marketing table with guiding principles in mind. And when it comes to effective B2B marketing today, we'd propose that there are three.

Here's the first: *Companies need to do everything in their power to keep the B2B relationship very, very personal.* Time was, B2B marketing could have just as easily stood for "belly-to-belly" marketing, an approach to sales that pretty much describes itself, if you can just imagine a backdrop of a baseball game, barbecue, or bar. Yes, of course, companies and their business customers wrangled over costs and delivery times. You don't place a $20 million order for, say, auto parts, or a $5 million order for cleaning supplies, without questioning every dollar in cost. But in the old days, B2B relationships tended to be collegial and long-term.

Then came a bunch of changes. Foreign competition, for one. Increased use of requests for proposals (RFPs) to get bids for another. But, when it comes to manufacturing at least, nothing shook up B2B marketing like the advent of online auctions, starting in earnest about 20 years ago. Suddenly, companies that needed 5,000 widgets could get suppliers from around the world to duke it out—and live, to boot. "You'd just sit there and watch the price collapse in front of your eyes," recalls Jim Berges, a longtime industrial products marketing executive whom we've known for two decades, and who's been in the business for twice that. "It was like overnight, companies could buy from China or India without going to China or India. It caused a feeding frenzy."

In due time, however, most companies came to see the limitations of online auctions. The price was right, and online auctions were good for some products—simple commodities, for instance.

But online auctions were not so good for many others. How do you put a complex, multi-staged, highly customized, multimillion-dollar project out to bid online, for instance? You don't.

Which leaves much of B2B marketing today back where it started. With marketers needing to forge deep, cooperative, long-term relationships with their customers. The kind of relationships that stop online auctions (and even RFPs, for that matter) before they start.

Like all relationships, such relationships have to be built on trust. With both sides feeling like they're in a win-win situation. "You have to give your buyers something—guaranteed quality, bundles of services, design input—that makes the savings of any auction just not worth it," as Jim Berges says. "You have to become a partner. You have to really know them, and they have to really know you."

In other words, for B2B marketing to thrive these days, it has to be eye-to-eye and brain-to-brain. It has to be personal and intellectual.

It also has to be ruthlessly strategic. The reason is simple enough: Sometimes partnerships just aren't profitable for the supplier in the equation. They don't make financial sense. Or maybe they do in the near term, but not in the long run, or vice versa.

Which brings us to our second operating principle. *Everything you do in B2B marketing today has to be driven by a careful analysis of industry capacity and capability.* Here's why. Because many industries are more consolidated today, with only a few suppliers and buyers in each, B2B marketing has become more like a chess game than ever before. Every move you make has to be taken with an understanding of its competitive chain reaction.

Take, for example, a story from Jim Berges about what happened a few years ago when a mega-retailer was in the market for new refrigeration units for all its stores. Such a massive order could only be handled by three big engineering companies, including the one where Jim was working. "Right away, the sales team wanted to be incredibly aggressive," he recalls. "That's the way it always is. The salespeople want to sell, no matter what."

But the "what" in this situation was important. If Jim's company got the mega-retailer's bid, it would kill his main competitor. Well, not kill it outright, but "steal" half of its business, freeing up its factories' capacity—with potentially dire consequences.

"Most of the time, in consolidated industries, you do not want a competitor on the scene with huge capacity and capability sitting idle," he says, "because they will most definitely retaliate on the next bid, which could be the business you *really* want from a profit standpoint."

The point is, in B2B marketing, you must pick your partnerships wisely. Consolidated industries have a way of heightening the trade-off between growth and margin, and when relationships tend to be few in number and long-term in nature, it usually makes sense to go for the margin. But you can only make that assessment when you're thinking strategically. In the B2B space, you cannot win every battle over a customer.

And you shouldn't want to.

Our final B2B operating principle mainly concerns industries that are not consolidated, and it is this: *Fear Amazon.*

Fear it, learn from it, adopt what you can from it—and fight it with all you can.

Look, there are still plenty of businesses that operate with big, thick catalogs as their engine. Catalogs containing hundreds, if not thousands, of small-ticket parts, widgets, and thingamajigs, and all the like. If you're in the building trades, you know what we mean. Nails come in about 6,000 varieties. Light sockets, same thing. The list is endless.

You'd think the Internet would have killed off B2B catalogs by now, but actually, in the industries where they're the most relevant, catalogs still account for about 60 percent of sales, mainly because there are a legion of buyers who still want and need to be able to pick up their phone, dial into a call center, and discuss their purchases with a real live person who knows a little something. Amazon, however, knows opportunity where it sees it, and in recent years it has been moving into this territory, using its usual tactics of killer pricing, killer shipping, and killer supply chain operations.

If you want to stay and play, your only defense is going to be killer service. Lucky for you, your employees have certainly felt Amazon's impact on their own lives, so they will intuitively understand why you are pushing them so hard for better performance. The enemy, so to speak, couldn't be more real.

Sure, you may be tempted to match Amazon's prices. But that's an unsustainable solution, for obvious reasons. No, you can only fight back by giving your customers more of what Amazon cannot. Expertise and guidance. Genuine interest and insight.

Yep, it's a partnership all over again.

As we said, B2B marketing has certainly been transformed by the new, interconnected online universe, only it's making it more like its former self than ever before.

Maybe not belly-to-belly, but high touch all the same.

Back in 1980, the renowned innovator Edwin Land was quoted as saying, "Marketing is what you do when your product is no good."

Land is no longer with us, and neither is the company he founded, Polaroid, ironically a victim of changing customers and technology, and most likely a product management team that couldn't find a way to keep up with either.

But Land's comment is still an excellent, if stinging, reminder that marketing has to start with a good product, be it in B2C marketing or B2B. It's even better if it starts with a great one.

Once you have that—and that's a lot—you can start to unleash marketing's full arsenal.

With consumer marketing, there's profitable accessibility—that's place. There's a well-tested, constantly refined cost proposition—that's price. Messaging that finds customers with laserlike precision and surprises them to boot—that's promotion. And an organization that deeply integrates marketing into every function—that's people.

With business-to-business marketing, there's the building of relationships in order to minimize auctions, buttressed by strategic thinking about capacity, capability, and your competition, including Amazon.

Either way, we might suggest a small revision to Land's quote.

Marketing, we would say, is what you do *after* you have a *good* product.

And today you can do more than ever.

7. CRISIS MANAGEMENT: WELCOME TO THE COLISEUM

If marketing in "normal" times didn't seem daunting enough, we now turn to marketing in bad times, otherwise known as crisis management. If you're lucky, you will never need the advice we're about to offer. But given the Roman Coliseum–like world in which we live, that's less likely than ever. It's as the *New York Times* recently noted, "Almost every day, the Internet demands a head on a platter."

And that warning doesn't apply just to big companies or top leaders anymore. Public relations crises strike all sorts of companies, new, old, and in between, for profit and not, suddenly throwing a harsh public light on people working at every level within them. You could be employed by your organization for two years when someone on your team—someone you didn't hire or even know—is found to have fudged the results of an important research report. You could be running a division in Chicago and get mired in a headline-grabbing scam perpetrated by a vendor in Atlanta. Crises were never just for the upper reaches of an organization, but once upon a time, your rank gave you cover.

Not anymore. Today, everyone needs to enter the arena with sword and shield ready.

Now, given the business we're in—speaking, writing, and consulting—we've obviously had many opportunities to opine on crisis management before. In fact, we devoted a whole chapter to it in our last book, *Winning*, published in 2005. And indeed, we'd make the case that our advice from *Winning* remains pretty unaltered ten years hence, with one caveat.

With the advent of social media, everything that happens to a company or an individual during a crisis happens faster now. Faster—and worse. Social media, for all its virtues—and we are enthusiastic users and consumers of it ourselves—does have a way of turning the world into a screamingly loud, brutally snarky echo chamber, with the propensity to ricochet bad news to Timbuktu and back more quickly than you can mutter the words, "Did you hear?" No wonder Monica Lewinsky once noted that the only good thing about her scandal was that it occurred before Twitter.

Twitter, and, of course, its social media brethren, don't change everything about crisis management, but they do warrant additional guidelines, which we'll get to soon.

Before we do, though, a quick review of our original principles of crisis management. For the sake of updating them, after each one, simply add the phrase, "Only it's faster and worse now."

First, no matter how hard you try to contain it, your crisis will get bigger and deeper than you think. Oh sure, there will be good days during your crisis—hopeful days—days when you think perhaps the story has run itself out. But the facts are, bad news goes on and on and on until every last detail of it has been exposed. Crisis suppression is, in a word, impossible. *(Only it's . . .)*

Second, there is no such thing as a secret in this world. Your lawyers may suggest you negotiate or buy silence from those involved in your particular crisis; your PR experts, too. But promises, contracts, and severance pay are imperfect solutions. If more than one person knows about your *mishegas*, you might as well put out a press release. Because when it comes to bad news, eventually everything will come out. *(Only it's . . .)*

Third, your handling of the crisis will be portrayed in the worst possible light. Go ahead, tell your side of the story to journalists. They may even seem sympathetic during the conversation; after all, it's their job to make you feel you've got a friend. But if you're in business and your organization is ground zero for a crisis, you are not going to get coverage that gives you the benefit of the doubt. *(Only it's . . .)*

Fourth, there will be changes in processes and people within your company because of your crisis. And by that, we mean there will be blood on the floor. Sorry to use such a graphic metaphor, but that's the way it goes. Crises demand change. Some of it will be good and healthy. New controls will be installed. A broken culture will be repaired. But in the process, the world tends to demand that one or more people pay for what went wrong with their jobs, and the clamoring of the crowds won't stop until they do. *(Only it's . . .)*

And fifth and finally, your company will survive its crisis, and become better and stronger having done so.

On this one, there's no need to add an addendum. It still stands. Because the facts are, most companies do survive crises, even terrible ones, and most do improve because of the experience.

Take Under Armour. It took a three-week social media excoriation during the 2014 Winter Olympics due to a controversy over the company's design of the U.S. speed skating team's uniforms, which many in the media blamed for the team's poor performance. Its stock took a hit and its CEO, Kevin Plank, took to the airwaves to fight back. Inside the company, the tumult must have felt absolutely life-threatening at the time. But somehow, the battle infused the company with new mojo. Under Armour double-downed on its relationship with the speed skating team, signing on to sponsor them through the next Olympics, and shortly thereafter burst out with a much-heralded new ad campaign and a slew of new products. Crisis, what crisis?

That said, yes, sometimes a social media pounding is so devastating that a company or an individual is crushed for a long time. Indeed, the list of companies and individuals deeply and perhaps permanently scarred by their crises is expanding every year. It would be hard to argue that business (or personal) mistakes are somehow getting worse. Businesses and individuals have always screwed up, flamed out, or otherwise blown up before the world's eyes. The thing that's changed is the multiplier effect of social media, which makes every error (or per-ceived error) spread faster, look uglier, and seem more egregious than ever before.

On a bad day, it can be enough to make you want to run your life from inside a cave.

THE PRINCIPLES OF STORM PREP

You can't, of course. You can't even try. It doesn't work, and indeed, most attempts at stealth in business backfire. There is no such thing as off the grid.

So, what then? Well, the most obvious answer is to try to prevent crises, and that's a huge part of what leaders are trying to do when they build healthy cultures with values that promote integrity and candor. And again, we don't just mean top leaders, but leaders starting at the team level.

Still, life happens. You're sitting around one day and suddenly your computer explodes with emails, or your phone starts ping-ing, or someone steps into your office and says she needs to talk to you right away. Something's gone wrong. Something import-ant. And in a heartbeat there's a big, fat, ugly mess in your back-yard. Or your front yard. Or indeed, right on your desk.

For that eventuality, we now turn to a set of communications practices to put into place for the good times, sort of like hurri-cane insurance. Such antidotes will not stop a storm from hit-ting, but they tend to facilitate the cleanup.

The first is to stockpile goodwill before you need it. There are lots of reasons for every company to be a good citizen in its community and lots of reasons for every company to be a fair, transparent employer. Add crisis management to the list. Having authentically earned friends and supporters in good times will increase the chances that you will have vocal defenders in the bad.

By the same token, some crises are personal, as in *you* have screwed up. *You* missed a huge deadline, lost a huge client, OK'd a huge advertising campaign that flopped. *You*, in other words, are the crisis, or at the very least, at its center.

Again, in such cases, the more goodwill you have stored away in the relationship bank, the better. Seeing yourself become a trending topic on Twitter is not the time to start thinking, "Who will vouch that I'm actually not the worst person ever born?" The time to start thinking that is the first day of your first job, when you pause briefly before taking your first call or attending your first meeting to remind yourself that yes, it's a known fact, everything that goes around does come around, or you stop to invoke Maya Angelou's similarly eternal truth, "People will forget what you said. People will forget what you did. But people will never forget how you made them feel." By your words and actions, make them feel like you're a good and decent person, too good and decent not to be defended by those who know you. It may not be enough to stop all the drubbing, but in a crisis, it may be all you have.

Another practice before the storm: have a robust public voice up and running on multiple channels, even if you have nothing very urgent to say. In a chattering world, you have to be a part of the conversation. In particular, if you're a consumer brand, a crisis is not the time to be meeting your followers or figuring out what your voice sounds like. Note here that we said "multiple channels." It's important to make sure your communications are occurring on every platform in good times, because when a crisis strikes, you can be sure your opposition will be busy defining and attacking you on any platform that you've left out.

The same is true if the crisis is personal. Everyone these days needs at least one direct-to-the-world channel for his or her voice. Twitter, Facebook, Instagram—take your pick. And don't think you're too "inconsequential" to the organization, or too "low level," to have a platform ready. In the worst-case scenario, you'll never need to use it. In the best, it will be ready when you are.

The best thing about social media in a crisis is that, despite its brutality, it does allow you to disintermediate your message. Gone are the days when you had to trust a journalist to get your message straight, presented in the tone you wanted, with the words you wanted. Today, no one has to stand between you and the public. You can speak for yourself. And if you're authentic enough and fast enough, and have your megaphone ready on every possible platform, that can work very well.

In 2013, when a prank photo showing an employee licking a stack of Taco Bell tacos went viral, consumer perception of the brand took a deep dive the very day the story broke. But Taco Bell took immediate action, firing the employee and setting the record straight on social media, ensuring customers that it was just a joke gone wrong; the food was never intended for con-sumption. The outreach worked, and the brand recovered to pre-crisis perception levels, as measured by YouGov's BrandIndex Buzz score, in just three days.

The point is: Taco Bell was ready to engage. Are you?

The next practice on the list: Don't accidentally create a cri-sis with how you let someone go. The truth is, many crises occur because managers do something really dumb; they actually create whistle-blowers and crusading critics. How? They fail to love departing employees as they exit the company. They fail to treat them with the same dignity on the way out with which they were treated on the way in. How humiliating that must feel. We discuss the right way to let people go in some detail in the next chapter on leadership. For now, just hold on to the thought that you must try everything to prevent an employee from leaving while feeling bitter. They'll live to remind you that stinginess—both financial and emotional—never pays.

Our final crisis management antidote actually only comes into play once a crisis has hit, and here it is. Hold tight to the one sure thing, that this too shall pass. Yes, in the thick of the crisis, the hating will feel horrible. You may fear losing your job, your reputation, your friends. The noise will seem unbearably loud and feel like it's lasting forever. You will feel as if everyone in the world is paying attention to you, and thinking about you, and dissecting you, and spending their every waking minute talking about you and your humiliating public mess.

Maybe they are. We'd posit that it's unlikely. But even if they are, know it will abate. It always does.

Listen: it always does.

The mob will move on. You can't control the timing. You can only control how much you let yourself believe things will never be OK again.

Things will be OK again.

Not by osmosis, of course. You or your organization, or both, must do what is necessary to remedy things. Fight back if that's what's called for. Make amends if that's the right path. Repair what is broken. Change the people or processes that went awry. Clean up, air out. Get back in the game.

But in all of that, don't let social media mess with your soul. Crises happen. You can prepare, and we highly recommend it. But even then, you may not be immune. So when one strikes, forge through with eyes open.

You'll be #oldnews before you know it.

PART TWO

IT'S ABOUT THE TEAM

8. LEADERSHIP 2.0

This is the chapter where we ask you to put aside (at least temporarily) the plethora of theories and platitudes you've heard about leadership over the course of your education and career, and entertain the possibility that leadership, very simply, is about two things:

1. Truth and trust.

2. Ceaselessly seeking the former, relentlessly building the latter.

In this chapter, we're going to take a close look at exactly how that's done, not from 20,000 feet, but from 20. Because leadership, for all the highfalutin stuff written about it, can't be an abstract exercise. It's in the details, or as we'll suggest, in the dos (and don'ts) of it.

But first, a short refresher, as we've opined about leadership before in this book. In Chapter 1, we made the case that work becomes a grind unless an organization's leaders have identified an inspirational mission and elucidated the everyday behaviors that bring it to life. We assigned a term to the critical connection between mission and behaviors—"alignment"—and asserted that alignment tends to happen much more often when people are rewarded for embracing the mission and furthering its success with their behaviors. (We called that not-too-shocking notion "consequences.")

Also in Chapter 1, we listed five essential leadership activities—essential because they're the spring rain and bag of fertilizer, if you will, of alignment. They were:

1. *Getting in everyone's skin*—caring passionately about your people and understanding what makes them tick.

2. *Serving as the Chief Meaning Officer*—using words and deeds to give your team's work context and purpose.

3. *Removing blockages*—clearing bureaucracy and other nonsense out of the way of your team's path to results.

4. *Demonstrating the generosity gene*—going over-the-top in your desire and effort to reward people for great performance, using money, promotions, and praise.

5. And, *making sure the work is fun*—creating an environment of enjoyment and celebration.

As we think you'll see, these activities are aligned with truth-and-trust leadership. Incidentally, the same holds true for the "Four Es and a P" framework we've used extensively in the past to talk about leadership. That framework asserts that the most effective leaders exude *energy*, have the skill to *energize* others, *execute* ideas in action, and possess the *edge* necessary to make decisions, all wrapped in a great big package of *passion*.

In our last book, *Winning*, we did what all authors do, which is we built a house on top of our framework, formulating eight rules for leaders. Looking over that list ten years on, we're happy to see they've all stood the test of time. Leaders still must relentlessly upgrade their teams, make sure their people live and breathe the organization's vision, and exude confidence and optimism. They still must act with transparency, have the courage to make tough calls, and ensure their directives result in action. And, without a doubt, they must still inspire risk-taking and take the time to celebrate victories large and small.

Here's the bottom line. Truth-and-trust leadership is one of those things in life that are greater than the sum of their parts. It's an overarching approach—an organizing principle—that drives everything leaders do every day, whether they're in staff meetings, performance evaluations, strategy sessions, or budget reviews, and everything in between.

Truth-and-trust leadership is a mentality and a methodology.

And in these times, it can and should be you, in action.

THE TRUTH AND NOTHING BUT

Truth is a good thing, right? Who's going to disagree with that?

Next to no one, probably. Not even the leader we heard about recently when a friend named Lauren called us for advice about a career crisis.

At the time, Lauren, 34, was a financial analyst who'd been working at the same small investment firm since she'd graduated from college. Her role involved research, and quite a bit of client service. Recently, the CEO of Lauren's firm had announced he was going to sell the business to its senior managers and retire, and in those conversations, Lauren had heard whispers that she might be made a partner as part of the transition.

But suddenly, the whispers stopped, and Lauren was informed (by a colleague) that her boss was the reason. She was stung enough to consider quitting. "They're going to lose a lot of business if I go," she told us. "The clients love me."

We asked Lauren if her boss felt the same way about her value to the firm. There was a pause, and then she blurted out: "He just doesn't want me to be a partner because I'm a woman. He got pissed-off when I went to part-time after my baby."

Was that the case? It's possible. But here's the story. Lauren was guessing. When we pressed her, she admitted she had no clue how her boss really felt about her performance, long before her baby or after, because he'd never told her.

What a shame.

A shame because regular performance evaluations are every manager's inexorable responsibility, but a shame too because if any of us were ever to meet Lauren's boss, say, at a leadership conference, surely he would agree with the hypothesis that speaking the truth at work is a very good thing.

Or take the case of a manufacturing company we know well. Owned for decades by a conglomerate that could only generously be called an "absentee parent," the company suddenly found itself the center of attention from its new private equity owners, who wanted to know every detail about how the business was run. Give us a talent review of your staff, they said, and paint us a vivid picture of the competitive landscape. How do we change our relative position? How do we change the *game*?

Hmm. Let's just say that if this exchange had taken place in a classroom, the manufacturing company executives would have been lucky to receive a grade of "incomplete." Why? Because for all intents and purposes, they'd stopped searching for the truth about their business years earlier, when their own bosses had stopped giving a darn. Like so many other people in business, they'd become accustomed to taking the easy way out, avoiding the kind of hard conversations and hard questions that seeking (and finding) the truth almost invariably involves.

Truth in telling people where they stand and getting very specific about how they can improve.

Truth in talking about how the business is doing and what real challenges lie ahead.

Truth in bearing down on the assumptions underlying a business's strategy, budgeting, and other processes. Every meeting, every encounter an opportunity to get at the truth of matters. Every meeting, every encounter ending with the reflection by all involved: "Did we get at the truth with our conversation?"

Take strategy. A few years ago, we heard Terry Leahy, former

CEO of the UK-based retailer Tesco, assert that strategy formulation is "an exercise in searching and searching for the truth." What a terrific way to put it. Indeed, the "Five Slides" process we described in Chapter 2 depends on truth-seeking analysis. What are the company's *real* capabilities? What does the playing field *really* look like?

These questions, if you want your strategy to amount to anything, must be answered with rigor. We hope that word puts a chill down your spine; it should. Rigor does not mean sitting through a PowerPoint slide by a manager you happen to like and nodding as he rattles off precise claims about market growth, competitive reactions, and new entrants. Rigor means asking, "Where did you come up with those numbers? What were the underlying assumptions that got you there? What kind of technology, from whom, could disrupt everything you're suggesting?"

Rigorous truth-seeking, as another example, does not mean buying into an HR presentation during a strategy review session that promises a new recruiting effort will yield results in six months. It does mean asking, "Is our pitch right? What companies out there are getting the people we want? What are they doing differently than we are? Are we fully exploiting LinkedIn's capabilities to mine good candidates? Have we offered our current employees bonuses to help us find industry talent? Just how competitive is our salary package?"

Ultimately, truth-seeking in strategy is just what it sounds like. A compulsion to never settle for suppositions and assurances. A hunger to dig and dig until truth, stripped of its spin, in all its glory or gore, is staring you in the face, whether you like it or not.

Now take budgeting. At the vast majority of companies, it's as "truth-challenged" a process as they come. Spin is everywhere; each group comes into battle with an agenda. Senior managers want fewer costs and higher revenue, and they'll dig, probe, and squeeze to get them. For their part, business units generally go into budgeting with a CYA defense. Their objective is to lower expectations in order to get bigger bonuses for exceeding them. They too will try anything to carry the day.

In the end, the numbers always end up somewhere in the middle, don't they? There's too little conversation about what's really happening in the marketplace, and not nearly enough about what would be achievable if people stopped bargaining and started talking about opportunities. The whole thing is a drill in spin and minimization.

It's amazing, though, how ingrained this kind of destructive budgeting behavior is. It can even happen in private equity, where private equity partners and their companies' senior managers are far more aligned than in your typical business environment. After all, in PE, partners and senior managers alike own a significant piece of the company, and there's no logical reason for senior managers to think they could enhance their careers by sandbagging the numbers. And yet, in our experience, it can take up to a year to 18 months for former corporate types to let go of their defensive, beat-the-budget mentality and get comfortable with talking honestly about how *together* both sides could grow their businesses faster.

But when they do, oh, the possibilities and positivity that unleashes. People start saying things like, "What if we take a hit to our second-half profits and invest in that new R&D project?"

and, "Let's talk about acquiring company X and company Y. Yeah, it may hurt in the short term, but it could be a huge hit down the road." Going private, with no external security analysts to please, should create an entirely new environment. Gone should be the days when budgeting was like a visit to the dentist for a tooth extraction. The conversations are all about choices, trade-offs, and opportunities. Rather than minimization, they're exciting exercises in maximization.

Exciting with a huge payback. Because in business, truth is a competitive weapon. It makes companies faster, fairer, more nimble, and more creative. It makes companies a place where people want to work, and a place where they contribute all they've got. Maybe you're thinking you're not high up enough in the organization to make truth-seeking your mantra. It's too risky; too different. Banish those thoughts. With its huge upsides, with the results it galvanizes, truth is for every leader, at every level, from first-time team leader to CEO. Sure, you can lead without it. The only question is, why would you want to?

THE TRUST DIVIDEND

We hope we've persuaded you that truth-seeking is leadership at its essence. But here's a reality you must face. You will never get truth without trust. People may not always want to hear the truth, but they tend to trust the people who deal in it, demand it, and display it at all times. So let's look at what it takes to build a foundation of trust in your organization with a list of leadership dos and don'ts.

The first "do" is to *care like crazy about your people and their work*. If this suggestion sounds familiar, it's because it's part and parcel with the five leadership imperatives from Chapter 1. Take demonstrating the generosity gene and clearing blockages as examples. Both are proactive, unmistakable ways to send the same message: "I'm in this with you."

The same point gets transmitted when you stand up for your people—in particular, when they're down. Look, it's easy to cheer on subordinates when they bring you a big, breakthrough idea or log a numbers-busting year. It's after the initiative flops that they need you to publicly own your earlier endorsement and take equal responsibility for its failure. Even in those cases when a team member has to go because he's fallen so short of performance expectations, he needs to be able to count on your managing the fallout with compassion and dignity. The trust-building "do" here, in other words, is to *have your subordinate's back when he's on his back.*

The related don't is one we've seen all too often: running for the hills after a subordinate stumbles on a risky bet you'd both agreed upon, all the while shouting over your shoulder, "I knew it wasn't going to work!" That's just ugly; it's the kind of cowardice that just reeks of self-preservation and it makes trust die, die, die in an instant. In fact, we'd go so far as to say that nothing destroys a leader's bond with his or her followers faster.

In a similar category is the claiming—or not—of credit. Have you ever known a leader who gathers up his subordinates' thoughts or initiatives (or both) and presents them to his bosses as his own? What jerks. If you're a leader who brokers in smart ideas—and who doesn't these days?—you must *celebrate ownership where ownership is due.* You'll get a reputation for integrity, and better yet, your people will be happy to bring you their best ideas.

Then there's the leadership "do" that you hear about all the time—listening. Listening, it's often said, helps leaders make better, more informed decisions, and of course, we concur with that. But we like listening as a trust-builder because it's a way to show respect for your people. One caveat, though. Listening is very important in the day-to-day, and effective leaders make it a common practice in routine meetings and the like. But what really builds trust is those times when you *listen when listening is hard to do*—during a crisis, for instance, when bad news is pouring at you as through a fire hose, or just the opposite, when you know nothing because the company's culture puts everyone in information lockdown. In such situations, people are on pins and needles. They're scared for their jobs. Sharing candor upward takes a massive dose of courage, really, and often, quite a bit of agonizing goes into it before the moment of truth. You, as leader, could hole yourself up in meetings with the powers-that-be, and otherwise isolate yourself from your team. It's only natural; you feel like every step you make might set off a land mine. And yet, it is in just such a situation that you must create opportunities for your people to share their minds with you. You may end up hearing the truth—something you desperately want, as we've said—or you may simply be available to absorb their emotions. Either way, listening to candor—*inviting* it—is part of your job.

Or take an acquisition, when suddenly you're installed as the new boss; no one knows you, and you know no one. Again, your people will be frantic, their futures unknown. For many, an acquisition is like a death; their whole world has been terribly upended. Then in you march. You could start barking orders and making unilateral decisions to demonstrate your authority. You could communicate upward only; after all, the stakes for you are very high. You could bring in your old team from your previous job and just take it from there.

Please don't. Be it a crisis or an acquisition, or another kind of mess, do whatever it takes to resist those impulses, and instead, make the time—hard as that may seem under fraught circumstances—to let people share their thoughts and perspectives and for you to reflect on them genuinely. You may not always agree, but giving people voice is the same as giving them dignity, a trust enhancer whose effects will last long after the crisis passes.

TRUST-BUILDING IN REAL TIME

So much of leadership occurs in meetings, doesn't it? Or it should. Meetings are where we gather to talk about work and how it's going to get done. They're where we share information about the competition, review products, natter about what's going on with technology, wallow in the week's numbers, and on and on. And yet, far too often, meetings are bland and predictable time drains, with each attendee giving a prescribed update filled with spin that everyone could easily read on paper. They're enervating maneuvers in nothingness.

But meetings are huge opportunities to build trust if you do them right—that is, if you encourage open debate and praise courage when someone says something bold, counterintuitive, or assumption-challenging, and further, if you reprimand the bullies who too often try to silence contrarian views.

Take the case of John, a Web magazine editor in chief we know who called a meeting not long ago to talk with his staff about "native advertising"—you know, those advertorials that look and feel like editorial content, and you often find yourself reading for a while before it dawns on you that they're not.

Now, journalists have a long tradition of hating advertising's intrusion on their noble enterprise, and John's hope with the meeting was mainly to tamp down a rising tide of anger against the organization's business side by promising that native advertising would never comprise more than 10 percent of the site's content, a deal that he had already negotiated with the CFO. This announcement was met with cheers from his staff, quickly followed by 15 minutes of native-advertising bashing. It was a veritable hate-fest. But then, just before the meeting was about to end, one member of the editorial staff, Liz, caught John's eye. His first good leadership move was recognizing that Liz was the only person in the room who'd been silent the whole meeting. His second was inviting her to change that. "Liz," he said, "we haven't heard from you. What's your take?"

At first Liz seemed to demur, but John pressed her again. After a pause, she relented. "Well, I actually disagree with all of you," she said. "I think readers are smart enough to know the difference between native advertising and editorial content, and I'd even go so far as to say, many people accept it as part of the online experience. They get its purpose."

The hush in the room was earsplitting, but in it, John urged Liz to continue.

She did, and then some. For years before becoming a writer, Liz had worked on the business side of another editorial site, and with John's quiet support that day, she gave her colleagues a sobering lesson in the economics of not using native advertising. She didn't appear to win over any adherents, and indeed, at one point, an outspoken member of the staff tried to silence her with a groan and rolled eyes.

John jumped in to chastise him: "Nick, knock that off," he said. "Liz just demonstrated something we need more of around here—candor."

John's last comment, by the way, is something we call "role model management," an incredibly powerful tool for cultural change, in which a leader specifically calls out (and holds up) an employee's behavior as a standard for others to admire and imitate. You can't deploy role model management often enough if you want to drive home the importance of certain behaviors. People really pay attention to public praise—and admonishment. Our main point here is about building trust through the encouragement of authentic debate. Imagine what would have happened if John hadn't encouraged Liz to make her case at that meeting. "John talks a good game about how we're a team," she might have thought bitterly, "but you're only on the team if you agree."

So use role model management—or use any means necessary. Just make sure people know no single voice controls the conversation in your organization. It wouldn't be truth-seeking handled any other way.

The risk of silencing open debate, we just suggested, is some portion of your employees feeling disenfranchised. A very similar dynamic occurs when leaders undermine trust by talking to subordinates about each other. This common occurrence—

basically, gossip by another name—is a massive don't. Yet it happens all the time because leaders are human, and being such, they become friends with some employees more than others. The next thing you know, you (the leader) are in your office with Sal, whom you went fishing with over the weekend, and you let down your guard, and you start complaining about Joe's performance. Now, Sal might—at first—enjoy the moment. He's in your inner circle! But after a while, unless Sal's not particularly bright, it's going to dawn on him that if you talk about Joe with him, you might talk about *him* with someone else, like maybe your other friends on the team, Lucy and Tim.

Hello, you've just created the trust environment of a middle school cafeteria.

Instead, the "do" here is to *keep confidences closely, and in public conversations and private ones, make it clear that everyone is on the same team*. That doesn't mean you won't be friendlier with some subordinates than others. Again, you're only human. But it does mean you can be trusted not to let friendship get in the way of fairness.

Along with gossiping about subordinates to each other, another leadership "don't" that really kills trust is having differing stories about the business for different audiences. The fact is, every leader is called upon to deliver status reports to different constituencies. It doesn't make any difference if you're a team leader and your constituents consist of (a) your boss, (b) three colleagues, and (c) a handful of clients, or if you're a CEO and your constituents include the board, Wall Street analysts, journalists, and so on. For any leader at any level, having multiple "concerned parties" is perfectly routine. What can't be routine is a substantive jiggering of the story for each group—a jiggering in emphasis, level of optimism, or data shared. Trust-building leaders *tell the same story to everyone all the time.* To do otherwise is a killer, especially now, when information has no boundaries or walls. Everyone hears everything, and variations or discrepancies or attempts at spin loom large indeed. So peddle in consistencies only, and enjoy the confidence in you that blows back at you from all quarters because of it.

Speaking of different constituencies, leaders also are often called upon to negotiate with such groups, from members of the local community, to vendors, to customers, to unions. It practically goes without saying that trust makes these conversations easier and more productive, but we need to say it because too often, leaders enter negotiations with what we refer to as a "too cute" mindset. They start with an unrealistic position or have a must-win attitude.

Look, negotiations with constituents require empathy. If you want to build trust, *get out of your head and get into the head of the other side.* See the situation from their perspective, with their history, their needs, their risks, their values. Ask yourself, "If I were sitting across the table, what would I want for myself or my people? What would be bugging me? What would I consider fair?" It is only with such open-mindedness—and openheartedness—that real dialogue can occur. Further, such behavior is an investment in future negotiations. If you've played fair before, your bargaining partner will expect it again, always a good place to start.

The final trust-building leadership "do" we'll mention here involves the unfortunate topic of letting people go. Obviously, no leader *wants* to fire an employee. Sometimes the employee has become a friend. Or they've been at the company for decades. Sometimes you worry the employee is going to file a lawsuit for a perceived injustice or join up with a competitor in retaliation.

Regardless of the specifics, letting someone go is almost always an unhappy and awkward situation that can rattle not just you and the ill-fated employee, but the entire organization or team.

If you're a leader, there is no faster way to exacerbate a firing situation than by distancing yourself from it. You don't want it to be your problem, but it is your problem. You must *own every departure*. You own the mistake you (or the organization) made in hiring the individual, you own your inability to coach him or her to better performance, and you own the responsibility for making the employee's exit as gracious as possible. Indeed, if you don't let someone go properly, not only does the employee lose trust in you; the entire team can, too.

So handle firings with care—extreme care. That doesn't mean dawdle and delay. In fact, one of the cruelest things you can do as a manager is to allow an employee to become a "dead man walking," hanging around the office while everyone keeps their distance, knowing the end is near. That's an agonizing bind to put a person in. Avoid it at all costs.

Now, if you've been conducting regular, candid, truth-imparting performance reviews, no employee should ever be surprised by the news that he or she must start the process of moving on. Indeed, in organizations with very effective feedback systems, underperforming employees typically have at least six months of advance warning, and with the organization's help, many find other work long before their time is up.

That said, such scenarios are woefully rare. Many companies tell people they are being let go and ask them to pack up their cubicles on the very same day. Except in cases of integrity violations, such a practice is terrible; we hate it. But whether that's the way it happens at your company or not, good leaders love every departing employee out the door.

That's right, love them out the door. In fact, love them on their last day as much as you loved them on their first, when you paraded them around to meet everyone because you were so proud of your great new hire. Sure, it might feel impossibly hard to summon up those emotions again; you must. Fight the urge to get mad at the exiting employee or to blame him or her for the situation. And for goodness' sake, even if the employee has been an underperformer, be as generous as humanly possible with severance.

In doing so, you demonstrate the kind of trust-boosting integrity that your departing employee will surely appreciate, and the keepers left behind will likely note with respect—and relief.

The funny thing about leadership is that before you're a leader, you're counting the minutes until you get the job. You're dying for the affirmation, the responsibility, and yes, even the "power" to get things done the way you want to—at last. Then you become a leader and within about two days, you realize how overwhelming the job is going to be. Yes, it's a thrill. Yes, it can be fun as all get-out. But then there's the employees who want and need your attention more than you anticipated. The competitors who are more numerous and faster than you knew. The budget constraints that don't allow you the flexibility you expected. The economic and technological disruptions that do not stop.

The only antidote is simplicity. The simplicity of leading through truth and trust. Ceaselessly seeking the former, relentlessly building the latter. In every decision, in every action.

Truth is a determined pursuit, a personal and unquenchable fire, burning to know what is really happening inside the company and out.

Trust is a muscle, strengthened by daily exercise. It is a discipline, honed in encounters with employees, superiors, and constituents of every kind.

Combined, the double helix of truth and trust cracks the code of leadership today.

9. BUILDING A WOW TEAM

I t's Monday morning. You're determined to create a truth-and-trust atmosphere all week in everything you do. That said, there are a few small problems you need to attend to immediately. You need to fill a key position that's been hanging open about, oh, six weeks too long, to the point of real work not getting done. And you need to do something—something *amazing*—to stop your best person from quitting to join a cool new tech start-up with headquarters in someone's cousin's uncle's garage.

We're talking blocking and tackling in this chapter. We're talking hiring and retaining.

We're talking teambuilding.

Look, every leader, new, experienced, and in between, knows that great results are the result of great teams.

Sometimes those teams seem to emerge spontaneously; everything and everybody clicks, like alchemy. But most times, team-building is a conscious act. It's a deliberate process. Let's look at its essential components.

HIRING 101

Great teams start with great players; that's why hiring is so darn important. Too bad it's so darn hard, too.

Why is it hard? Two main reasons. First, some people interview like pros, but implode when faced with the real work on their desks. But most times, the problem is you, Mr. or Ms. Manager. You screwed up. You hired for X skill and what you really needed was Y. Or you failed to notice a team-killing personality trait the candidate happened to have in excess. Happens all the time. In fact, in our estimation, getting hiring from the outside right more than 60 percent of the time, and promoting right from the inside more than 80 percent, puts you in superhero territory.

Since hiring right is so tough, it's important that you don't get all caught up in your knickers when you make a hiring mistake. Skip the embarrassment part. Think of it this way: you've just joined a very large club, the "But I Was *Sure* the Candidate Was Perfect" Association of Gobsmacked Managers International. (We are both members ourselves.) Admit your hiring error, and please, stop doing the new hire's work for him or her in order to hide your mistake from your own boss and peers. As with any "crime," the cover-up is always worse than the original offense. Believe us, your bosses have walked in your shoes, and you'll be respected for facing into the truth. Own up to the mismatch, move the unsuccessful candidate out quickly and with dignity, and start again.

Start again better. Start again with the right kind of checklist.

You do have a hiring checklist, right? Most managers do. The problem is, because hiring can be so daunting, over time many of us develop checklists that read like a history of our mistakes, composed of the qualities we missed, as in, "For God's sake, don't forget self-awareness next time. Arthur was so clueless about himself, he drove everyone insane!"

We're not going to hate on your checklist. If you've been hiring for a while, it's probably pretty refined. We're just here to tell you it's not enough. It's not *precise* enough.

Good hiring checklists—the best ones—are inextricably linked to your organization's mission. Deeper still, they're linked to the *specific skills and behaviors* that you've ascertained will achieve that mission. Yes, we're talking alignment again. Of course we are— because alignment is the freshet of success; it's the river's source.

Now, we understand that there are a number of "must-have" traits that most managers look for in the hiring process. Integrity is one of them, and of course, you want it on your list. It's a simple "go–no go" prerequisite, no matter how attractive the candidate is on every other front. Also in this "must-have" category, the widely popularized components of emotional intelligence: self-regulation, self-awareness, internal motivation, empathy, and social skills.

Fine, fine, fine. But along with all those admirable qualities, you must—repeat: must—hire for the carefully identified, do-or-die skills and behaviors your organization needs to achieve its mission. That's our biggest message when it comes to hiring, and we cannot stress it enough. Hire deliberately.

Remember in Chapter 4, on globalization, when we made the case that people managing overseas operations today truly need one key trait to succeed? It was discernment, which we defined as the combination of business savvy, cultural sensitivity, self-confidence, and the good old wisdom to know when to push forward the company's will and ways, and when not to, out of respect for local customs and mores.

Now, imagine your company has overseas expansion as part of its mission. What are you going to look for in your hires? This is not a trick question; yes, the answer is a big, whopping dose of discernment.

By means of another example, in Chapter 1 we talked about CEO Dave Calhoun's turnaround of Nielsen, the global market research company. Dave explained that Nielsen's reinvention was made possible by installing a largely new cadre of people, all of whom embraced the three behaviors that he and his top team deemed necessary to transform a big, lumbering, silo-ridden media conglomerate into a fast-moving, highly integrated organization in the business of measuring the ever-changing patterns of consumer purchasing. The first behavior to support the mission was open-mindedness to new ideas, the second was a strong propensity to share those ideas across organizational boundaries, and the third was a capacity to simplify the vagaries of big data for colleagues and customers.

Without a doubt, Dave hired people with all sorts of other

traits as he rebuilt Nielsen—candor, compassion, energy, and on and on. But we guarantee you that most everyone had the big three he needed. Nielsen wouldn't have done so well otherwise.

Successful hiring takes discipline; that's it. It takes *knowing* the particular skills and behaviors that your particular organization needs to win, *probing* candidates to see if they possess them, and signing on *only* those people who do. And here's the thing. You still might miss now and again; hiring's like that. But up your odds with rigor. Good hiring demands the opposite of winging it.

As with every pronouncement like the one we just made, there are a few critical addendums and caveats that go along with it. Sort of an "uh-oh" folder to carry with you during the hiring process, if you will. Ours would contain the following notes.

- No matter which three or four or five mission-driven skills and behaviors you have on your hiring checklist, make sure the list also includes IQ. In today's business environment, the playing field isn't level. It is tilted toward the team with the smartest people.

- Personality matters. Especially a bad one. There's a great story about Bill Clinton—he tells it himself, in fact. Every time he gives a speech, he says, there might be 10,000 cheering people, but he'll invariably home in on the lone grump in the crowd, and he'll spend every last minute until he leaves trying to make that person smile.

Glum, annoying, overbearing, phony, or other-wise unpleasant people always seem to have a way of drawing attention to themselves, don't they? And in a work setting, they can bring a whole team down. Obviously, if a candidate possesses *exactly* the dazzling technological capabilities you cannot live without, you might make an exception. But, man, should that bar be high. While you can't train negative energy out of a person, a person—yes, even one person—can sure infect your organization with it.

• Certain industries, and in particular, the creative industries, contain a higher than normal quotient of—how can we say this?—drama-seekers. You know, the people who love spectacle, in particular with themselves at the center as the main attraction. Unfortunately, such people tend to be very talented, or else they wouldn't so often end up as candidates on your short list, with you thinking, "Hmm, I really like Bob, but he seems extremely . . . emotional."

The problem with excess emotionality is that it expands to fill the space available to it, spawning junk like palace intrigue, gossip, and repeated per-sonal dilemmas. People get married and divorced. They buy homes. Most employees know how to han-dle these life events with the proper amount of shar-ing. Drama-seekers can't go through them without an audience. Sometimes their talents are worth the cost in lost productivity. But not often.

- Next, be on alert for any person who doesn't get that he's, well, just a person. We're talking about a surfeit of self-confidence. Don't get us wrong. Healthy self-confidence is a must-have, as it's the font of resilience. But when it seems like someone you're interviewing for a job might have the propensity to swell instead of grow, that's an arrogance high alert. Stay away.

- Finally, your uh-oh list needs to include the question, "Did I check the candidate's references—like, did I *really* check them?"

  Yes, of course we understand that many reference checks are BS. Either the candidate has handpicked someone who's going to spew superlatives—why wouldn't they?—or you end up with an executive who gives you the usual CYA, "We don't discuss former employees" line.

Don't leave it at that. Bust your butt to find someone who really knows the candidate. Then listen—to what is and *isn't* being said. If you're getting blasé commentary or lack of detail about achievements, do not hold the phone away from your ear, though it will be tempting. Fight also the urge to make excuses for your candidate. ("That company is a mess; they didn't appreciate Kathy.") You must face into references, especially the bad and the ugly. If you don't, three months after Kathy starts to flail on the job, the person at whom you'll be yelling, "I told you so!" will be yourself.

THE PLACE TO STAY

Let's turn now to your employee who wants to go work in a garage. Or in a loft in San Francisco. Or at your biggest competitor. In other words, let's turn to retention.

Tomes have been written on retention, but we don't really get that. Retention is very simple. It's a matter of happiness. Happy employees are engaged with the work, they're challenged the right amount, they like and sincerely care about their coworkers and customers, they're motivated to do well by both, they're productive, they collaborate and cooperate and thrive.

They stay and they play.

Right? So all you have to do is make sure your employees are having fun. That they're filled with hope about the future, for both their careers and the company. That they're fulfilled, challenged, and inspired.

Their happiness is your job.

Please, do not over-brain this imperative, or forget where it starts.

It starts with money.

Look, money matters to people; it matters a lot. Of course it does. You cannot eat prestige. You cannot send your kids to college on free snacks in the lunchroom or casual Fridays. That's why, as a manager, no matter what level you're at in your organization, you need to pay generously and based on performance. It's a baseline requirement for both motivation and retention—that is, happiness—and yet it's amazing how many leaders forget this fact, especially the higher they go in the hierarchy. Don't do that. Though it might have been years or decades ago, hang on to that feeling you had in your chest at your first raise, your first bonus, your first stock option. The excitement. The sense of possibility. The feeling of belonging. And hang, too, on to the day you found out about a lousy raise, or the bonus you didn't get that you thought you deserved, and how disconnected those events made you feel.

If you're a new boss, hark back to the generosity gene we described earlier in the book. Maybe you weren't born with it, but it's never too late to claim it as your own. Love giving out raises, even if your own wasn't as much as you wanted or expected. Go ahead anyway and share in your employee's happiness; after all, you're on the same team.

As impactful as money is, thank goodness it isn't the only tool you have to increase your people's happiness quotient.

You've also got "wow."

Yes, "wow." By which we mean a fun, exciting, empowering *environment*. An environment where people want to come to work.

This is not a directive, by the way, for your boss, or your boss's boss. "Wow" is *every* manager's responsibility—if you're managing a team of three, or an army of 3,000.

OK, how's that done?

The first step is understanding that, sooner or later, you will lose many of your best people to entrepreneurial ventures unless you offer what they do, short of a jackpot payday: positive energy, a "we might be giants" kind of ride, the opportunity to speak up and be heard, the chance to make a real impact, freedom from stultifying, stupid bureaucracy, and its common cohort, meaningless, busywork-making layers.

You will lose your best people, that is, unless you have a culture that's not about shutting people down; it's about setting people free. A culture that offers immediate responsibility, fun, and significant financial upside for outsized results. A culture where no individual feels like a cog, and everyone understands the meaning of their contribution. A culture where great ideas that don't work are admired for the effort rather than punished. A culture where people can be promoted for performance before they've logged the requisite hours in a dues-paying assignment. A culture where people don't have to navigate labyrinths and salute little generals to get anything done.

A culture, in short, that unleashes people to feel and act like owners.

We know such vibrant cultures can be hard to inculcate in big, old-line organizations, but they're not the only fortresses. We've seen stultifying cultures (or pockets of them) in just about every size and type of company. And we understand that companies, especially larger ones, need controls, especially in today's post-Enron, post-financial-industry-meltdown economy.

You just can't let controls undermine your creation of a "wow" place. Instead, use truth and trust to unlock people's ideas and ungum processes, and use role model management, too. When someone is adding to the fun and excitement of your team, sing their praises loudly. And when someone is sucking the wow out, call him out on it at the same volume.

At the end of the day, what you want as a leader is to create a team that's like the house of that kid you knew in high school—the house where everyone wanted to hang out because it was where all the fun stuff and action were. Where your friends could always be found. Where you didn't want to go home for supper.

You know what we mean. Make your place a place where people are happy, and you'll be happy, too.

THE (NOT AT ALL) TERRIBLE TWO

Even if you've already developed a wow culture, here's some good news: you can do still more to build great teams. You can differentiate, and you can empower HR.

We say this knowing, of course, that differentiation can incite certain people to riot, and HR is often seen as uncool.

No offense, but wrong and wrong.

Differentiation first.

Briefly, differentiation is a performance evaluation system that's the embodiment of truth-and-trust leadership. At least twice a year, every employee meets with his or her manager. The manager puts in front of the employee a simple one-pager, preferably hand-written so it feels more personal. In the left column, the manager lists what he or she likes about the employee's performance, and on the right, where they could improve. There's then a conversation about how the employee is doing in terms of hitting his or her goals, strategic or financial, and how well they're demonstrating the company's key behaviors. At the end of the conversation, the manager gets very specific. "Joe," he says, "you're a superstar. You're in the top twenty percent of our team. Your future is bright here, and we're going to increase your salary with a bigger-than-average raise to reflect how much you contribute and how long we expect your runway to be. Thank you." Or he might say, "Joe, you're doing pretty well, but there are some skill areas you really need to develop, and we're eager to help with that. You're in the valuable middle seventy percent of the team, and your raise will reflect that reality." Or finally, he says something like, "Joe, it's not looking good. As we've discussed, you've been missing your targets for six months, and you don't share ideas, one of our most valued behaviors. You're in the bottom ten percent, and there will be no increase in your pay as we go forward. Let me assist you in thinking about how to find a better-fitting job within the next year."

Now, critics of differentiation, and they are rabid, often call it by a different name, "rank-and-yank," and complain it's "cruel" to the underperformers asked to leave, and subjective to boot. Our response is, really? Really? We'd say differentiation is actually empowering. It allows employees to break out of the darkness of uncertainty that is all too common in companies with lousy management, and take control of their futures.

It's terrible, but such transparency and empowerment are rare. Over the past decade-plus, we've had hundreds of opportunities to ask crowds, "How many of you know what your managers think of your performance?" On a good day, 20 percent of the audience raises their hand. On a typical day, it's closer to 5 percent. Can you spell "demotivating"?

Another criticism of differentiation is that it's an anathema to teamwork. With only so many places in the top 20 percent, the argument goes, everyone will try to destroy each other as they claw their way in. Except it doesn't happen that way. Recall that differentiation is based on an employee's performance around numbers *and* behaviors. All a manager has to do is identify that teamwork is a valued and rewarded behavior. You can't be in the top 20 percent unless you demonstrate it. You can't even be in the middle 70. Then guess what happens? That's right. Teamwork on steroids.

But forget the critics for a moment. It's hard to know how many of them there are, anyway, as their rancor may actually outweigh their numbers. Let's get down to the really important thing about differentiation, which is how it unleashes wow by creating a meritocracy.

Good people are attracted to meritocracies. That's just a fact of life. Smart people, talented people—they know their worth, they want to win, and they like to hang around with people who share those sentiments. They yearn to work where their worth will be acknowledged in the pocketbook and the soul. No star performer, for instance, wants to work where he or she earns the same as some disenfranchised lout in the next cubicle who's just slogging along. It feels unfair because it is unfair. It's downright enervating.

Now, we realize that differentiation is not perfect. No performance evaluation system is. But in our experience, differentiation is the best out there. Its clarity is liberating. It unleashes excitement and opportunity. And for good people, that's a reason to smile—and to stick around.

A NEW CONSTRUCT FOR HR

There was a story in the *New York Times* in 2013 that reported that a preponderance of Silicon Valley companies go without HR departments because they're seen as "the enemies of speed and efficiency." Unfortunately, Silicon Valley, with a few notable, high-profile exceptions, isn't alone in its anti-HR vibe. But we are here to promise you that HR isn't optional—not in any industry. And every CEO and top team needs to buy into that reality. Without good HR, people development tends to fall through the cracks, and that's dangerous. People development is integral to people happiness.

Now, let's not be Pollyannaish about this. We understand why HR gets a bad rap. It gets a bad rap because most organizations lump administrative HR and real HR together.

That has got to end.

By "administrative," you know what we mean. The part of HR that puts employees on the payroll, arranges your security pass, and handles benefits. In a perfect world, as we see it, this part of HR would not be part of HR at all; it would be subsumed or otherwise owned by the finance department. Such an arrangement would liberate real HR to do what it is meant to do.

In such a construct, HR directly reports to the leader, and is composed of a healthy mix of seasoned HR professionals and savvy, people-oriented managers drawn from all functional areas. A former plant manager with hands-on labor experience would be a great part of the HR team, for example, as would an individual with years of experience running the company's district sales unit.

The point is, HR has to be filled with street cred. Rather than being speed bumps, they're welcome partners with their front-line managers and peers, using their ability and insight to challenge management to identify star performers in the top 20 and promising ones in the middle 70, and design training opportunities and challenging assignments to keep them engaged and growing. They also work with the bottom 10 percent, easing their transition to other employment, simultaneously making sure the bench is always full, so that any important role can be filled from within the ranks quickly and successfully. In sum, HR has nothing to do with administration. It's about people, pure and simple—finding, training, motivating, and retaining great talent.

Does that sound optional?

To us, it sounds like the bedrock of an organization where teambuilding is a top priority, and where good people feel excited to contribute and committed to stay because their careers matter to someone besides themselves.

We realize, of course, that the kind of HR we describe sounds like CEO-only territory, and often it is. But if you run a small company, or you run a division of a large one, or say you're starting a business—all of these situations can present an opportunity to get an HR person on your team. And if that happens, grab it. Pluck an individual from sales or manufacturing who's proven his or her aptitude with people, someone who has that street cred we just mentioned, and make them the HR leader whose sole job it is to help build a great team. You won't believe the impact.

Impact right where it matters, too: on how your people feel about their work, their careers, and the company itself. No matter what level manager you are, your people's growth, development, and, we'll say it again, their happiness, are on you. Let HR help you carry the load.

Nothing good in business happens when you're alone on the field. As we said earlier, it's the ultimate team sport.

That's why you have to get the right players out there with you. First, by hiring for skills and behaviors with discipline, rigor, and a carefully curated, mission-driven checklist to match. Hiring is hard enough as it is; improvising only makes it harder.

Once you've got the right people, you need to create an environment that motivates and retains them. That happens when you work diligently to rid your culture of bureaucracy and politics, and imbue it with the kind of innovation and opportunity that unleash people to care and contribute as if they were owners.

It happens, too, when you use differentiation to remove the cloak of uncertainty from performance, giving employees and managers alike the power to control their destinies. Meritocracies rock.

And finally, it happens when you release HR from administrative minutiae to do its real job: identifying talent, building careers, and helping to forge the kinds of teams that change lives and companies.

Put these practices together, and prepare to be wowed.

10. GENIUSES, TRAMPS, AND THIEVES

Remember 1971? Probably not, for many people reading this book, and honestly, we don't remember it with any notable precision ourselves. Richard Nixon was president. China was a closed fortress; Japan was launching its assault on America's consumer electronics business. Gas cost 40 cents a gallon, and computers were as big as houses.

It was also the year that Cher dominated the music charts with "Gypsies, Tramps, and Thieves," the song from which the title of this chapter is derived. Cher, incidentally one of the most lasting artifacts of 1971, was singing about a wandering band of outcasts. In this chapter, we're writing about quite a different group of outliers, actually three groups, united by one thing.

They're particularly challenging to manage.

First, not gypsies, but "geniuses"—those individuals whose work you don't understand, or couldn't do yourself. These employees generally dwell in a stratosphere of technical complexity; think coders, analytics experts, or engineers, or any employee whose brain is a black box to you. It used to be that such employees were pretty rare. By the time you were boss, you'd done most jobs on the way to the top, or had been exposed enough to them to understand their fundamentals. Today, you can rise through marketing or finance—heck, you can be an English major at Duke, as in one of our examples—and find yourself managing scores of techies whose output can make or break the organization.

Next, "tramps"—those individuals who largely work from home, or who are freelancers or contract workers. Let us be clear: we mean no disrespect by the use of the word "tramps"; it's just meant to connote the untethered, peripatetic nature of this group. They're on the team, and often, they're important contributors; they're just not *there* there, but rather are out of sight, and too easily out of mind.

And finally, "thieves." Elsewhere in *The Real-Life MBA*, we talked about employees who commit integrity violations, and our bottom line, we hope, was unmistakable. Such individuals must be dealt with swiftly, severely, and publicly. There's no point, to quote ourselves, in penalizing bad behavior in private.

Here, however, we're not addressing those kinds of thieves. We're addressing something much more commonplace: employees who steal your time and energy, underperformers and inveterate conflict-creators. You probably won't be surprised to learn that we take a pretty hard line with such productivity-drains, but you might be surprised to hear what we consider the most dangerous "thief" to stalk any organization. It's not a type of employee, actually. It's a feeling—fear. Fear of job loss, fear of industry collapse, fear of economic decline. If you're a leader, part of your job is acknowledging that many of your people live with worry as their constant companion. And it's your job, too, to face it straight on.

OPENING THE BLACK BOX

Joey Levin remembers his first day as CEO of Mindspark, a software developer that builds, markets, and delivers dozens of desktop applications for consumers, including Television Fanatic, Translation Buddy, and Coupon Alert. It was 2009, and Joey had, to that point, spent his career in M&A, first at Credit Suisse, and subsequently at the media company IAC/InterActiveCorp, Mindspark's parent. But there he was, the new leader of a software company employing several hundred software engineers.

"I will never forget the look on the face of the CTO when we met; let's just call it very skeptical," Joey recalls. "He knew more about tech than I would ever know in my lifetime, and we both knew it."

They shook hands.

"I have a lot to learn from you, and I look forward to learning from you," Joey said as an opener.

"*You* want to learn from *me*?" the CTO asked his new boss, incredulous.

"Yes, because I don't understand what you're doing, and I want to."

At that moment, Joey recalls, everything changed. "I actu-ally remember his face going from skeptical to relieved and very open," he says. "It was like this moment of realization that we could work together, and that's exactly what happened."

Today, Joey runs a $1.6 billion division comprising several IAC businesses (including Mindspark), but his early partnership with the CTO at Mindspark still serves as an excellent example of how to manage "geniuses" so that everyone wins.

It's truth and trust all over again.

The truth part starts with the understanding—from both sides—that there can be, and will be, no mystery about the work. That means managers will be expected to ask, and ask, and ask, about the work until they understand it on some level, and that "geniuses" will be expected to keep answering, and answer-ing, and answering, until such time, and not begrudgingly, but eagerly.

Sometimes this kind of truth-seeking means the work has to be broken down into component pieces, small and graspable. Joey Levin cites the example of an acquisition he worked on before Mindspark, where the CTO informed the top team that the com-pany urgently needed a new data center. Price tag: $100 million.

The request was unexpected, to put it mildly.

So the management team began digging, going over the pro-posal with the CTO, chunk by chunk. "Why," they asked, "do we need to own the building?" "Why does the building need to be located where you say it should be?" "What kind of hardware goes into the building?" "What impact will each piece of hard-ware have on our desired strategic outcomes?"

That last question—linking the work to strategic outcomes—is particularly important in truth-seeking. After all, IT "geniuses" can be just like every other kind of functional expert. They want all the bells and whistles they can get for their special projects. The difference is, when other functions ask for money, it's usually easier to understand what they're talking about.

To make a long story short, the truth-seeking exercise at the acquisition resulted in a $20 million IT investment, not $100 million, and the company was no worse off for it. In fact, Joey says, the smaller solution ended up being more flexible and productive.

As for the trust part of managing geniuses? It comes, as Joey Levin learned his first day at Mindspark, with showing respect. It also comes from having high-brain experts who also happen to have the right values.

"The best tech people are bilingual," Joey explains. They speak fluent tech; they're the real thing. But they also speak fluent business. They embrace the company's mission and values. They understand what activities drive revenues and costs. They worry about the competition. They feel strong ownership of the numbers.

It's fine if your top product person is a tech savant, Joey adds, the kind of visionary who floats above the practicalities of P&Ls and all the like. But his or her boss? No. Tech managers have to care about deadlines, bottom lines, and product lines. They have to be practical and analytical.

"The best CTO is a person who wants to be a CEO someday," Joey observes. "They don't come to the table to negotiate, padding the numbers so you meet somewhere in the middle. You're on the same team."

Another terrific example of managing "black box" employees comes from a man we'll call Roger, the English major from

Duke we mentioned earlier. Roger, who's 34, runs a high-tech audiovisual design and installation company in Atlanta, managing 45 people who somehow know how to make music, TV, and Internet all instantly and perfectly available throughout complex commercial building projects. Most of his employees have advanced degrees in sound engineering and music technology.

"I have no idea what they know," Roger readily admits.

Like Joey Levin, that doesn't stop Roger from trying to find out. "I ask a lot of questions," Roger says. "I want to show them how much I want to learn from them, and how much their work interests me, because it really does."

But Roger considers gaining tech expertise a small part of his job. The bigger piece—the more important piece—is building a team that's unified around the company's foremost strategic goal. "The number-one thing I care about, and the team needs to care about, is creating a great customer experience," he says. "In some cases, when people come to us, they've just had a disastrous experience with another vendor, or with one of our older systems. In other cases, we're solidifying a good relationship. Either way, it's about better connecting us with our customers."

To achieve that, Roger is practically a textbook example of the teambuilding practices we've talked about in this book. He gets into his people's skins, he cares passionately about their lives and interests. He strives to make meaning of their work.

"I try every day to give them the big picture, to explain why the company is doing what it's doing, and why embracing that change is going to be great for them and the customers," he says. "My job is to keep the team motivated and inspired. I see myself as the manager of people loving it here."

Yes, part of that role is about understanding the work. But it's also about understanding the wor*ker*.

"I think my team can see that I sincerely care about them as people," he says, "and so everything I say about the work, they feel is coming from a place of trust. And that helps us get a lot done together."

In the end, then, managing geniuses is not all that different from managing mere mortals. Don't let their unique skills get in the way of an authentic relationship, one built on truth and trust. After all, geniuses are people, too.

STAYING CONNECTED (ON STEROIDS)

The going estimate for the number of Americans working from home is one in five, but you sure would have thought it was more than that in 2013, when Marissa Mayer, the CEO of Yahoo, banned the practice from her company. "To become the absolute best place to work, communication and collaboration will be important, so we need to be working side-by-side," she explained at the time. "That is why it is critical that we are all present in our offices."

Well, well, well. Marissa might as well have gone on to insult puppies and rainbows, given the outrage. Yes, some people supported her; we were among them. In our experience, you can't lead a turnaround without your people in the room. But in general, reactions to the Yahoo decree—at Yahoo and elsewhere—ran along the lines of, "I can't work any other way," and, "You can't turn back time. This is the future of work."

We're not going to use this space to make a case for the

"Everyone in 9-to-5" model of work. Virtual employees are here to stay. Indeed, the same research that put the number at one in five Americans working at home also predicted that figure would increase 60 percent over the next five years. (The study was conducted by the Telework Research Network, and cited in *Forbes* magazine.) It also noted a similar trend with freelancers and contract employees, who tend to work remotely, and in many cases, have several other clients: that cohort grew from 10 million in 2005 to 42 million in 2013.

So, what are managers to do to keep their more far-flung people in the game?

The answer: unleash every tool you've got to maximize socialization, which we define as those interactions that make sure the culture and spirit of your company, and its values and behaviors, are demonstrated and transferred. Socialization cannot happen haphazardly, either. It has to be a *real* priority, enabled by technology, and executed with unflagging intensity.

As a poweful example, we can draw on our experience with the Jack Welch Management Institute at Strayer University. Our MBA program, which we founded in 2010 and now help lead, is fully online. This format perfectly accommodates our 900 students from around the world, all of whom are working professionals who don't have time to travel to a campus or the flexiblilty to take synchronous terrestrial classes. Indeed, our school is so virtual, the only time students physically come together over the course of two years is at graduation.

While we do have a team of 30 professionals managing JWMI's operations from Strayer's headquarters in Herndon, Virginia, our faculty is almost as far-flung as our students. Forty professors, all with a PhD and many with MBAs as well, teach their classes from all over North America. Some are full-time, working only for JWMI; others are part-time, with second jobs as consultants or business leaders. They are responsible for lecturing about course materials, actively participating in class discussions, grading papers and projects, and generally making sure students are both contributing to, and getting as much out of, their classes as possible, so that JWMI can fulfill its mission of "Learn it today. Apply it tomorrow."

The challenge of managing JWMI's dispersed educators falls mainly on Dr. Michael Zeliff, JWMI's associate dean of faculty. Mike has had a career in academia and business, and he's drawn on both experiences to create a host of best practices to enhance socialization.

The first is a customer relations management–like (CRM) process that takes the randomness out of communications between Mike and each faculty member. We won't go into the details here, as they are many. Suffice it to say the process systemizes daily calls, emails, Skype sessions, and the like, so that no teacher goes without personal contact with Mike every week. Sometimes that contact is long—a visit on the professor's home turf, or an hour talk on the phone, for instance—and sometimes it's a 15-minute check-in. But every single week, every single educator in the field has a high-touch socialization experience with Mike. And once a month, the faculty of each department has a scheduled, Web-enabled meeting to discuss curriculum development among themselves. This session, which Mike facilitates, can last hours. Again, socialization in action.

Obviously, Mike's communication with the faculty is not

limited to scheduled contact. As is to be expected, emails fly back and forth all day, and when needed, conference calls or Web-enabled meetings are quickly arranged. But our point is, socialization cannot be left to such incidental interactions. They're not enough. Socialization takes intentionality.

A second technique that Mike uses to manage JWMI's faculty is a dashboard that feeds him with a constant stream of data about how professors are performing in their classrooms—how often they comment on student remarks, how long it takes them to grade assignments, how often they log into the online classrooms, and so on. This data is always calculated as a ratio, so that Mike can evaluate how faculty members are performing. For instance, the dashboard might show that a marketing professor is in the top 10th percentile for frequency of comments on student work. But it might also show that the professor's comments are in the bottom 15 percent for length. Such data allows Mike to have more meaningful socialization conversations with his team, whether they are part of the CRM process or more spontaneous.

A final practice that Mike uses to manage JWMI's virtual faculty is a little untraditional when it comes to academia, but we've found it to be catalytic: every semester, JWMI students rate their professors before they receive their grades. Teachers who bring the material alive and who interact frequently are rewarded in the soul and the pocketbook. Those with middling performance are coached, and those with poor performance are put on probation. This application of differentiation, we've seen, is an extremely powerful way to reinforce the right behaviors. As an added benefit—and it's a big one—this faculty rating system incents our faculty to socialize with each other. Everyone, it turns out, wants to get on the phone with the professor who gets the highest marks on student engagement, or talk with the professor who gets high scores on "use of visual media." As Mike puts it, "In my career, I've known plenty of professors who've seen each other every day and never exchanged a thought. They just wanted to do it their way. The funny thing is, in managing a virtual faculty, we've found that we can have professors all over the world who want to build a team that's always sharing ideas."

We love what's happening at JWMI, but great examples of socialization techniques are everywhere. Sue Jacobson is the CEO of Jacobson Strategic Communications, a thriving firm in Philadelphia with one full-time employee, Sue herself, and a team of about 42 contractor workers who have specialties from pitching the media to crisis management. Sue draws her team mainly from the ranks of working mothers who have traded in corporate jobs for freelance flexibility.

While Sue's business model works well for clients and for her own bottom line, several years ago she realized it did little to give her freelancers the sense of community that many of them missed by working at home, or to enhance the kind of learning that's so important for growth. In response, she instituted Tuesday morning "lightning round" meetings, during which every freelancer currently on assignment has five minutes to talk about her project.

"These are not show-off meetings," Sue says. "We don't let that happen. They're for sharing and brainstorming and helping each other out."

They also happen to be one of the best parts of the job for most of Sue's employees. They love the camaraderie and the advice they often receive, so much so that Sue thinks the lightning rounds are a key reason why she's kept such a stable team. As we all know, freelancers come and go, following the work and the money. In five years, Sue's lost only six.

Again, the reason is socialization.

Socialization—when it comes to managing "tramps," that's the word that should be ringing in your head. Use technology in all its glory to stay connected, and make it intentional. Out of sight can never be out of mind.

THAT GIANT SUCKING SOUND

Some employees literally steal from your organization, but as we've said, they're rare, and as we've also noted, managing them is straightforward. A big, loud, public kick out the door.

By contrast, employees who steal your time and energy are much more typical, but for some reason—guilt, maybe?—they're some of the hardest to deal with.

Let's start with underperformers, those team members whose work consistently puts them in the bottom 10 percent. By definition, differentiation would tell you that managers should spend very little time and energy on these individuals except to ease their transition to other work; after all, the vast majority of a manager's efforts should be devoted to hugging, supporting, and otherwise cheering on the company's stars, its top 20-percenters, and advising and coaching its valuable middle 70.

Why does it almost never go that way? Instead, most managers find themselves in countless productivity-sucking meetings and sidebar conversations about underperformers. "Rick didn't finish the spreadsheet again, and Sally had to stay up all night so we could have it for the clients. What are we going to do?" "Clare missed another deadline, but I don't want to push her on it because she said she had a migraine." "Ralph is killing everyone's morale with his constant jokes about bankruptcy. Who's going to shut him down?" And it's not just the conversations, either. The biggest energy drain with thieves can often be the effort it takes to push past their caveats and excuses, and goad them into doing the work in the first place.

Stepping back from almost any situation with an underperformer, it's always easy to see the solution. They need to move on—sooner rather than later. Up close, however, organizations tend to draw out departures, as people fret about the employee's emotional reaction to being let go. Oftentimes, managers feel guilty about putting a friend out of work, or remorseful they didn't give candid enough feedback along the way, or both.

And so, they dawdle and delay. They meet with HR. They toss and turn at night. We have a friend who's the CEO of a family real estate development firm with about 300 employees. He told us he spent an entire summer trying to work up the nerve to fire a man we'll call Harry, who had been with the company for 40 years, and was ensconced as head of special projects. Many considered this individual to be "the soul" of the company; he'd just been around for so long, and he loved to regale his colleagues with heroic stories about the early days, when it was just him and the CEO's dad working out of a basement apartment. But the CEO and his top team knew the man hadn't really done his job well for a decade.

"I cannot tell you how many meetings we had in the boardroom to discuss Harry," our friend told us. "We worried what would happen to him when we told him. We worried how the organization would react. We talked and talked and talked, and no one could face into what we had to do. It was paralysis."

Finally, after a summer of stalling, the CEO called Harry in and asked him to retire by Christmas. There would be a grand party and a generous severance. The door would always be open.

Much to the CEO's surprise, Harry wasn't surprised himself. He was grateful for the graceful exit. Even more surprising to the CEO was the organization's response. Nothing short of jubilation. Yes, people liked Harry. They appreciated his contributions to the firm's history. But everyone had done the calculus. His departure was long overdue.

"I cannot believe how much I was distracted and weighted down by Harry's situation," our friend told us. "As soon as he was gone, it was as if I suddenly had swaths of free time to pay attention to the business. I wish I'd done it five years ago."

That's our advice to you, too, if this story sounds even vaguely familiar. The most valuable resource you have as a manager is your attention. Invest it in top people and those with the potential to join their ranks.

The same recommendation goes for inveterate conflict-creators. You know the type we mean. The people who consider it part of their job—or their persona—to disagree with just about everything and everyone. Now, sometimes these individuals are very useful. They challenge the status quo; they hinder group-think. And a lot of times they're pretty good performers to boot. Indeed, they consider their results their shield. You can't let me go. I'm too valuable.

Again, such employees tend to steal time and energy, and

not just from their managers, but from everyone, as meetings devolve into discussions of their objections or opinions. As a manager, you just cannot let this happen. Some conflict is good, but pushback should be coming from every member of the team. When it's coming from just one to the point of distraction, it's time to say goodbye. Keeping an inveterate conflict-creator on the team doesn't make you a good, balanced manager. It makes you a robbery victim.

THE PARALYZER

Finally, let's talk about something people in business generally hate to acknowledge: fear.

Long gone are the days when people thought their jobs were guaranteed for life, and their companies and industries secure for the future. All of us have seen people—even talented people—laid off. All of us have seen companies go under in a matter of months, and whole industries collapse.

In the brave new world of global competition and economic stagnation, fear will always be with us.

It is part of your job as a leader to manage that reality. To talk about what your employees really need to be afraid of, and what's just rumor or conjecture. Because if you don't, we can assure you that their imaginations will take them places where very little productive work gets done.

We know a regional retail manager we'll call James. For six years, James saw his career soar as he helped his team increase sales almost 10 percent annually. But then James's boss—the general manager—was lured away to a fast-growing online competitor. Her first move? A call to James asking him to join her team.

"She went right for the jugular," James recalls. "She told me we were going under in a matter of months, given what she'd heard from her bosses before she left. She said that's why she'd bolted. She suspected our whole industry was in trouble because we were primarily brick-and-mortar and our customers were buying more and more online, where we were struggling to get a presence."

For days, James could barely function at work. Was the organization really close to collapse? If so, why wasn't the CEO talking about it? He knew the industry was in a lull, but everything he'd read convinced him it would rebound.

James started to speak with his colleagues about his concerns. It was a natural response, but one that started to spread like a contagion. Soon, every time a few employees were together the topic was sure to bubble up. Was the company in trouble? Were layoffs coming?

James's fear was generated by a person with an agenda—his old boss on a raiding expedition—but fear can be spawned by any number of sources. News reports, analysts, competitors. It doesn't matter. Management's response needs to be the same.

Absolute candor. About each person's performance and professional trajectory, the business's financial condition and growth prospects, and your best understanding of the industry's future.

The fact is, the absence of such information doesn't make people more focused on their work. Ignorance at work, about the work, is not bliss. Ignorance is an invitation to wallow in worry, an unproductive activity if there ever was one.

Franklin Roosevelt was right. The only thing we have to fear is fear itself. As a leader, your job is to slay fear, ceaselessly speaking the truth, in good times and bad.

We are not going to conclude this chapter by talking about Cher again, although we're happy that her song title gave us a framework to talk about three groups that operate somewhat outside the "tent."

Geniuses are a cadre of employees growing in number and importance. Then there are the virtual-ites, working from home or the road, sometimes full-time, sometimes freelance, and also growing in preponderance. And finally, there are the time-stealers, some obvious (like underperformers), others less so, like conflict-creators and uncertainty.

You now have an arsenal of tactics and techniques to manage all three categories. Pepper your geniuses with questions; dig and dig more. At the same time, show them you care; get to know them as people. Break projects into small parts to make them understandable. With remote employees, get deliberate about communications; install processes and technologies that maximize socialization. And with the thieves, fight back with courage and candor.

Not surprisingly, all of these practices add up to truth and trust. Ceaselessly seeking (and speaking) the former, relentlessly building the latter. Ultimately, it doesn't make any difference what kind of person you're managing, does it? Genius or average bear, virtual "tramp" or cubicle dweller, fearmonger or fear absorber, people need a leader who knows how to take fellow travelers and turn them into a team.

PART THREE

IT'S ABOUT YOU

11. WHAT SHOULD I DO WITH MY LIFE?

Over the past decade-plus, we've written a lot of columns about business, and by a lot, we mean upwards of 500. The topics have ranged from the perennial, like the principles of leadership, to breaking news events, like Joe Torre's contract with the New York Yankees. Some of these columns have received general agreement; others have incited *&!#-storms of controversy. But few of our columns sparked the kind of emotionality of "Four Reasons to Quit Your Job," which, in short order, generated more than 750,000 views and nearly a thousand heartfelt and heartbreaking comments.

Too many people sit at their desks all day wondering, "What the heck am I doing here?"

Yet, by their own admission, most stay put. Inertia is the culprit in some cases. In others, people lack the career opportunities to leave unhappy job situations, or they face lifestyle constraints, or both. As one commenter put it, "In these years of recession . . . you have to bear whatever the situation is at your workplace."

But too many people stay in get-me-out-of-here jobs because they don't know what else they should be doing with their lives. All they know is that it isn't what they're doing at the moment.

Sound familiar? If so, read on, because the goal of this chapter is to help you make that problem go away.

A DATE WITH DESTINY

A few years ago, we were part of a Microsoft-sponsored online series called *It's Everybody's Business*, in which we visited one company per episode and helped its management team work through a problem that was vexing the organization. It was during this diversion—which was really fun, by the way—that we ended up at Hertz, advising the company on the launch of its hourly car-share service, then known as Hertz Connect. (It is now called Hertz 24/7.)

In the process, we met a 42-year-old Hertz executive named Griff Long. It would have been very hard to miss him. Griff's energy was kinetic. Sort of like the Incredible Hulk, he always appeared to be on the verge of bursting out of his suit. We soon learned that Griff, when he wasn't making the case to senior management that he should run Hertz's new venture, was running, often as much as 20 miles a day, after which he'd go swimming and biking. On weekends, Griff competed in triathlons or coached others who were training for them.

Griff did eventually end up in charge of Hertz Connect, but the assignment didn't last long. We report this as great news, and Griff would, too. Because Griff left Hertz to take a job at Equinox, the upscale fitness lifestyle brand. His days now consist of opening new club locations, meeting with Equinox's managers and their top trainers, and talking about ways to encourage more people to exercise more often.

For the Equinox job, Griff had to let go of his concerns about salary advancement, and moved his family 1,500 miles away. But, he reports, "My happiness is huge and my wife and kids are so much happier, too. I never feel like I'm working. I'm doing what I was born to do. My only regret is it took me twenty years to get here."

Don't we all know stories like Griff's? The doctor who quits her job at age 50 to become a photographer? The corporate senior executive who jumps ship to run a museum or go into academia? The basic narrative is always the same, too—years or decades of "captivity," traded in for a second chance at living authentically, topped off with a moral of the story about doing what you love.

Such stories of reinvention, of course, are to be applauded. Similarly, trying on different jobs (or even industries) for a couple of years before settling on a career trajectory is normal and necessary. It's healthy exploration.

What pains us is Griff's long delay in finding career karma. Twenty years!

That's so common, but it doesn't need to be—because an antidote exists. It's a career assessment process called Area of Destiny (AOD).

Here's how it works. Imagine your life as two superhighways. One courses with the stuff you're very good at, the other with the stuff you really love to do. Now, imagine those superhighways intersecting. Right there—at the overlap of your capabilities and your happiness—lies the site where ideally you should build your career.

Whoa, right? Who does that?

Well, Griff Long did—eventually. But like Griff, most people begin their careers without an AOD as their goal. Instead, most people pursue careers based on what they're vaguely good at in school, like an A-student in political science becoming a lawyer, or a top English student going into publishing. Or they take a parent's suggestion along the lines of, "There are lots of jobs in technology these days," or, "You never have to worry about a paycheck if you're an accountant." Or they grab an offer that's expedient because it will, say, allow them to live at home for a year or two or work in the same city as their significant other.

In concept and practice, AOD blows up that kind of momentum-based career *mishegas*. Let us emphasize that word "momentum," too. It's such a common reason things happen in life. Where we go to college. Where we end up living. And yes, where we go to work. AOD gets in the way of that; it's a momentum antidote, one of the best we know. It impels you to think about who you are and what would make your life abundant in meaning, impact, and happiness. To quote Mark Twain, "The two most important days in your life are the day you are born and the day you figure out why."

AOD is all about expediting that second day.

Maybe that's why an AOD assessment isn't particularly easy

to conduct. You've got to dig. You've got to grapple. You've got to be brutally honest about your skills, capabilities, and values. You may even need to do a bit of soul-searching.

Take the first superhighway—*the stuff you're very good at.* That doesn't mean the stuff you're pretty good at or somewhat good at, OK? Such a list, for most people, would be reasonably long. I'm good at writing presentations, you might think. I'm pretty solid at math. I'm good at getting things done. Whatever. Hordes of people in this world, thanks to decent parenting, education, and inborn gifts, are generally competent.

So forget that. The power of AOD lies in the word "very." What are you better at than the majority of people? In fact, what are you better at than *most* people?

When that's the question, your answer has to become refined. "I'm particularly good at turning complicated scientific concepts into plain English," you might say. "Everyone's always complimented me on that." Or, "I'm terrific at math when it comes to analyzing the cost and profitability of a new enterprise." Or, "I'm very good at getting things done as part of a team under extremely tight deadlines, and I'm even better at it when no one likes each other because I have a real knack for building consensus."

Over the past few years—we started using AOD analysis around 2010—we've heard all sorts of granular answers to this question. One woman—a classics major in college reluctantly thinking about a career as an academic—finally came up with, "I'm incredible at making strangers feel welcome. I've always been told that. And I guess it's true." She's now very happy as an administrator at an American university's study-abroad campus in Greece. A headhunter in his mid-twenties (already having a career crisis brought on by, in his words, "intractable bore-dom") offered, "I am uniquely good at connecting with really screwed-up kids. They gravitate to me—and I gravitate to them. They need to talk. I like to listen." He ditched his job on Madison Avenue to work at a wilderness education program for troubled high school students.

We cannot overestimate the importance of taking the time to identify the skill, capability, or trait (or two) that really dif-ferentiates you from the pack. Reflect on your life experiences from school to camp to family situations to jobs. When did you *particularly* excel? In which situations did you make the *most* impact? Was it as a peacemaker, a negotiator, a listener, a per-suader, an analyst, an inventor, a critic, a facilitator, a competi-tor? The list of possibilities is as endless as the human capacity for excellence.

Figuring out the "stuff" of the second superhighway is some-what easier. People tend to know quite spontaneously what they love to do because they rarely get to do enough of it. But to put some rigor into this process, think about your calendar for the next week or month or year. Which activities are you looking forward to more than anything else? Which fill you with the most excitement, expectation, and even joy? Presenting a new business plan to your team? Sitting alone or with a close advi-sor, musing over a strategic decision? Meeting friends for a long dinner? Volunteering with children at a local school as part of a company mentoring program? Traveling to places you've never been? Again, the list of possibilities is long, and you may love to do a slew of things, but for the sake of conducting a good AOD assessment, you need to narrow your picks. Which activities, undertakings, and pastimes really turn your crank?

With the two "superhighway" questions answered, all that's left with AOD is figuring out what industries, companies, or lines of work exist at your superhighway *intersection*. Sometimes it's obvious, sometimes not so much, for the simple reason that life, with all its many financial and personal constraints, can get in the way.

For Griff Long, it was the former. Here was a person who was excellent at sports and helping others become athletic in a very organized, very disciplined way. He was also a person whose favorite thing in life was participating in sports or talking about training with other sports fanatics. After decades working in the car rental business, no wonder he looked like he was about to implode when we met him. He was spending the bulk of his waking hours engaged in a desk job that was an imperfect match for his skills and didn't come close to filling his (emotional) cup. Fortunately, there was a whole industry that did.

By contrast, take the example of an acquaintance we'll call Jim, for whom figuring out how to land his career in his AOD intersection was more confounding. Jim studied musical theater in college and, after graduation, moved to New York to pursue a career on Broadway.

As with countless other hopefuls, Broadway didn't happen for Jim, and so after two years, he went back to school to become a landscape architect. Why? Well, he'd always been good at drawing, and he liked being outside. Plus, it felt like steady work. It was, he told himself, a good-enough solution.

Indeed it was, for 15 years. Jim got his degree, landed a job at a good firm, made junior partner, married, and had two kids. On weekends, he "indulged"—his word—his musical theater heart by singing in his church choir.

But something was missing. He knew it. His wife knew it. And that "something" was professional fulfillment. It was excitement. It was hope.

Enter AOD. Using the technique, Jim was able to pinpoint that he was very good at something that sort of surprised him: bringing teams together. In college, he recalled, directors used to fight to get him involved in their theater productions. Something about his upbeat, no-drama manner (in a world teeming with literal drama queens and kings) had smoothed out differences and galvanized people to work together productively. Jim's architecture bosses had noticed this gift as well; whenever there was a tough client or logistical or personality complications, he was assigned to the project.

As for the stuff he really loved to do? Well, besides spending time with his family, Jim just wanted to sing all the time.

Overlap, you might be thinking, what overlap?

But with some creative thinking, Jim identified it himself—musical theater management. He wouldn't get to sing every day, but he'd be around singing, which was almost as good. And in the meantime, he could really make a difference getting the hundreds of moving pieces involved in every show to come together.

Jim was thrilled about the outcome of his AOD assessment—"It feels so right," he said—but he also knew change wouldn't be easy due to financial obligations. He figures it will take five to ten years to segue from landscape architecture to theater management. Such time frames are not unusual for people whose AOD assessments reveal a far-flung "intersection." Indeed, sometimes getting to your AOD may not seem possible at all; it requires too much upheaval. Still, we would suggest that just knowing your AOD is useful, if only to give you a North Star.

A final AOD success story illustrates the disruptive (and positive) power of this seemingly simple device one last time. It concerns a young man we'll call Marcus, who attended college with every intention of majoring in geology. Why? Because in high school, Marcus had been good at math and science, and as careers in those areas go, geology seemed the most interesting. Plus, he'd heard the energy field had lots of jobs.

Freshman year was not even half over when Marcus discovered what it meant to be "*very* good" at math and science, and he knew one thing for certain: he wasn't. Marcus had also learned that a career in geology meant graduate school, and he was bereft thinking about six or seven more years of struggling to stay even with the pack. But right around then, he bumped into his AOD, or to be more accurate, he bumped into a worried set of parents who came bearing the AOD process.

The trio set about determining what Marcus was uniquely good at, and the answer came quickly. It was music, and more specifically, identifying new music that was going to become popular in a couple of months or a year or two. An obscure skill, perhaps, but one that Marcus had exhibited since he started listening to music as a kid. He often featured "about to be famous" music on his weekly radio show, which he started at age 14 and continued to host through college. In fact, it was a family joke that Marcus could predict Grammy Award winners three years before they were nominated.

As for what Marcus loved doing—that too was a no-brainer. It was listening to music. He also loved talking about music, sharing it with friends, reading music blogs, and going to concerts, the more unknown the band the better.

Today, Marcus is headed toward a promising career as a music programmer. To say he is happy is an absurd understatement.

His parents are happy, too. We know because we are them.

Anyway.

Look, there are a multitude of career books out there, containing a multitude of assessment tools. We don't mean to reinvent the wheel, just to offer the most effective way we personally know to answer the question, "What should I do with my life?"

Spend it in your Area of Destiny. It's where achievement meets happiness. It's where work stops being work and becomes life in all its fullness.

MORE THAN A LIFESTYLE

Some of you reading this book may not remember the olden days of yore, when being an entrepreneur wasn't what everyone said they wanted to do. But such times did exist, back when dinosaurs roamed the earth. Or more seriously, back when careers pretty much happened inside skyscrapers or other similar buildings filled with people in suits. In the 1970s, the oil crisis had people rushing toward degrees in geology. Energy was where the action (and the money) was going to be! In the last 30 years, investment banks and consulting firms have been the MBA employer of choice, attracting newly minted graduates the way a vacuum sucks up cookie crumbs off a rug.

For most of the last decade, entrepreneurism has been having its moment (or two or three). To be clear, this dynamic isn't particularly widespread. In fact, as the *Wall Street Journal* recently reported, Federal Reserve data from 2013 indicates that the share of people under the age of 30 who own private businesses has reached a 24-year-low. But it's also a fact that a certain start-up-or-bust zeitgeist has taken hold at many top business schools. At Stanford, for instance, it's considered something of a badge of honor to not attend any recruiting interviews; why bother, if you're starting your own thing? And at MIT's Sloan School, one of us (Jack) taught a class where roughly one out of six students had started a business before even graduating.

Why such enthusiasm? Well, being an entrepreneur looks insanely fun, doesn't it? It looks heroic. You write the rules and there are no rules. Your office is in a warehouse; meetings are conducted at the foosball table. You work like an animal for a few years, but then one day, it's you ringing the bell on the stock exchange. A few years later, you're acquired, and after the trip around the world and the purchase of a professional sports franchise, you start all over again.

Now that's living!

But there's one catch.

To be an entrepreneur, *you need an idea*. A big, fat, value-adding, mind-blowing, paradigm-shifting idea. You need a different and better idea than all the ideas already out there.

And there's a second catch, too.

Along with that idea, you need a rare kind of fearlessness. We're not talking about a run-of-the-mill tolerance for risk, or even an above-average tolerance. To be an entrepreneur—a *real* one—you need the cold-blooded courage, crazy passion, and irrational determination to endure the repeated near-death experiences that will most definitely occur along the way to making your idea a reality. You might run out of money a few times. You will make dumb mistakes. You will have suppliers and partners who flake out on you. You will not sleep. You will not want, need, or get a chance to.

What we're describing here is guts. And to be fair, most people understand that part of the entrepreneurial equation. What most don't seem to understand, in our experience, is the "big idea" part. Indeed, in our travels since 2001, we've met hundreds, and probably thousands, of individuals (particularly students) who've excitedly told us of their desire to become entrepreneurs, only to balk when we then ask, "So what's your one-of-a-kind product or service?"

Sure, there've been occasions when an answer shoots right back. An industry-changing way of selling consigned clothing online, for instance. A handheld medical device to treat migraines. We heard about both of those ideas in their infancy from their founders and got goose bumps. (Today, incidentally, both companies are up and running.)

But more often—much more often—we hear something like, "Idea? Well, I don't have one yet. Maybe a new app. I'm not sure.

But I *am* sure I want to be an entrepreneur. I just don't want to work for someone else."

That yearning, while completely understandable, is not enough. That's the bottom line here.

Please note, however, that our admonishment, if it applies, doesn't mean you're doomed to corporate drudgery for the rest of your life. All it means is that you probably shouldn't start something yet. What would you start? But you can certainly look for work in an entrepreneurial environment.

Remember Bunny Williams, whose story we told in the chapter on globalization? After a long and successful career as an interior decorator, Bunny decided to launch her own furniture line in 2010, with pieces manufactured in Asia and distributed in retail outlets around the world. Bunny's better/newer idea was that, by working closely on quality with Asian craftsmen, she could find a way to mass-produce upscale, designer-label furnishings and sell them to aspirational homeowners at moderate prices.

Bunny also knew what she didn't know: how to finance inventory, and how to do the books for her new business, for example. She immediately started filling out a team of experts in each of these areas around herself.

If you're an entrepreneur-wannabe without an idea, you can be part of such a team. Think of how many entrepreneurs-in-waiting got their starts working at high-tech success stories over the past 30 years. That's your kind of in, and it's a great one. To this day, Bunny credits her team with her venture's success. "I knew what I could do, which was all about the design. Everything else, I turned to them. They taught me so much."

Sure, as a member of the team, you don't share in all the glory, or the equity, of a start-up's founding idea-generators. But when the moment comes to commercialize your own big idea someday, you'll be ready. You can't put a dollar figure on that.

YOU CHOOSE

No chapter about careers would be complete without some discussion of a subject commonly called "work-life balance." After all, whether you do an AOD career assessment or use some other tool, in making a choice about what you'll be doing with most of your waking hours, you're also making a choice about what you won't be doing, or will be doing less of, in your nonworking hours.

Notice our use of the word "choice." That, in a nutshell, is why we prefer the term "work-life choice" instead of "work-life balance." In our mind, the former term acknowledges that every career decision carries consequences, which the "decider" understands and accepts. By definition, "balance" implies that a certain split is ideal, and it's around 50-50.

Here's the thing. A 50-50 balance *is* ideal for some individuals. True, it's not for us. Because we happen to think work is wildly fun and we work together and we're sort of intense, we go more for an 80-20 or 70-30 split ourselves. But again, that's a choice. It's *our* choice. We wouldn't want people telling us how we should spend our time, and we don't take any pleasure in telling others how to design their lives.

Basically, we think this whole thing is about values—personal values. An individual who values intellectual discourse, learning, alone time, and deep friendships with one or two people is not going to make the same work-life choices as a person who values money, fame, and being invited to a lot of parties. Similarly, a twenty-something brand manager who dreams of becoming a corporate CEO by the age of 40 and loves the emotional high of skydiving on Sundays is not going to make the same work-life choices as an MBA drawn to nonprofit fund-raising because of the flexibility it will give him to help raise his children.

Again, who's to say which values are right or wrong? Not us. If someone wants to go for something like a 50-50 work-life "balance," along with all its consequences, power to him or her. Same with 20-80 and 80-20.

And yet just go out in public and try to say that. We did, and we got slammed.

It was 2012, and we were asked to speak at the *Wall Street Journal*'s "Women in the Economy" conference in Palm Beach, Florida. We had no agenda going into the event, and we surely had no intention of generating OMG headlines and snarky blogs, but that's exactly what happened when we made the "work-life choice" argument you just read. More specifically, we said success in the workplace was a function of overdelivering on results, taking on difficult assignments, and demanding consistent, thorough reviews from your managers in order to gauge where you stand. We also said that taking a reduced schedule and asking for limited availability in order to tend to family (or other interests) was a perfectly fine choice, but it was not going to accelerate anyone's ascent to the corner office, *male or female*.

Well, talk about igniting an online onslaught of, um, unfavorable comments.

But then, a funny thing happened. A number of prominent women CEOs said they agreed with us, some of them very publicly. And just like that, the controversy went away.

So, here's to defusing this topic. Work-life choice isn't about anything but exactly that . . . choice. Every career decision you make has consequences. Social, economic, emotional. Those consequences need to line up with values—*your* values.

Everything else is just noise.

Look, the world has its share of people who know exactly what they want to do with their lives.

We wish that kind of fulfillment for everyone. And it pains us that it can be so elusive.

That's why we recommend the Area of Destiny technique with such gusto. It's a catalytic mechanism for getting you from the dire and lonely place of, "What should I do with my life?" to the energized, encouraging territory of, "I *love* what I do with my life."

So dig deep. Analyze and assess. What are you really good at, what do you love to do, and what unharvested field of dreams lies at the intersection of the two?

Should the answer to those questions point you toward an entrepreneurial route, we urge you to keep digging more. Do you have a big new idea? Do you have the guts to start something new? If not, what young and daring venture might you join until your spectacular *aha* arrives?

Finally, we urge you to dig deep to understand what kind of "balance" you want in your life. Is it 50-50, or something different? And just as important, ask yourself, "What are my choices and their consequences? Do they jibe with my values?"

After all, the person living the answer to those questions is you.

12. GETTING UNSTUCK

Along the way in life, almost everyone has encountered the depiction of purgatory from Dante's *Inferno*: a vast, waterless pit filled with forsaken souls frantically searching for a way out, particularly in an upward direction.

Grim, right? And familiar-feeling, too, if your career has ever stalled.

You're an individual contributor who wants to run a team. A functional expert who yearns to move into general management. A middle manager who thinks you're overdue to get P&L responsibility. But when you ask about timing or push the point with your boss or HR, the answer is always, "Not yet, not yet. Just hang in there."

But you've been hanging in there for what feels like an awfully long time.

It's soul-killing, that waiting. You love business, and you're sure you can do more. You may even feel as if you're in your Area of Destiny. But like the inhabitants of Dante's netherworld, you feel stuck.

Do not despair.

The truth about purgatory (the career kind here on earth, that is) is that it always ends. At some point, if there's no movement, out of your mind with frustration, you jump. You take a lateral move within your own organization just for the get-out-of-jail momentum of it, or you quit for a position at another company that's better for the main reason that it's not your current job. Or, in some situations, a career stall ends because your company loses patience with you, and bit by bit, or all at once, you're pushed. None of these are especially appealing scenarios. We get that.

Which is why this chapter is about forging another path, one that leads to the promotion you've yearned for.

Will it be easy? Probably not. But you can make it happen. The process starts with understanding why your career has stalled—*really* understanding. After that, you have six options for action. You can attempt all of them, but two or three of the options might be enough to break your impasse.

It goes without saying that no one loves change, and several changes at once probably sound like as much fun as sunbathing in the Arctic Circle. But Dante had it right about purgatory: "Here indeed may be torment," he wrote, "but not death."

You just can't let that line describe your life.

WHY CAREERS STALL

Every career-stall story has its own particularities. Its mitigating factors; its extraordinary circumstances.

But generally speaking, careers only stall for a few reasons, which we're going to run through here before getting to the action steps that we believe might help turn your situation around.

First, careers can stall when your company does not have a position for you to grow into. There's a "blocker" above you—usually your boss—who's doing a fine job and has no plans to retire, change industries, or move to Toledo. Your boss may even have a blocker above him or herself. Such a situation can be absolutely maddening, but it happens all the time in business. The main culprit is lack of growth; your company, industry, or the economy overall is in a hard place, standing still or even contracting. In such situations, opportunities for upward mobility are necessarily hard to come by. But blocking is also endemic to family companies, where the top jobs are often filled by certain "preordained" individuals.

If you're in a blocker situation, you really only have one choice, and it's to decide how long you're willing to endure stasis. And we mean, *decide*. Put an expiration date on your patience. "If something doesn't change within a year, I'm putting out feelers, and within two years, I'm out of here," you might conclude.

In this assessment, you also need to consider your standing within the company. If a promotion becomes available, are you likely to get it? Have you been getting A-plus performance reviews or only in the B range? Do you have an embedded reputation that might be hard to shake? Is your boss known for promoting his or her best people or sitting on their careers while he or she reaps the benefits? Every piece of such data is critical in determining the terms of the "perseverance contract" you write with yourself.

Importantly, there is no rule on the right amount of time to wait out a blockage. All that matters is that you explicitly pick a time frame based on your values, standing, circumstances, and constraints, as well as your company's future. In doing so, your stall won't end, but with a clear horizon and potential exit plan, your daily angst will surely ebb.

Another general reason that careers stall is wrongheaded notions about the importance of multifunctional expertise. We see this phenomenon all the time. Mary is a terrific financial analyst. Jeff is a star in marketing. Back in business school, both Mary and Jeff were repeatedly assured that the fastest, smartest, most time-tested way to senior management was by successively seeking out and landing stints in every function. "You need two to three years in each function, plus some time in international," they were told. "You need to build a well-rounded portfolio of competencies."

How cockamamie. Yes, there are some companies that like to parade their high-potentials through the fairgrounds, stopping at every ride. But far more often, companies promote people who are known to be really, really good at what they do, and they promote them right up the ladder, all the way to the top. The facts are, if you're a finance guru, you don't need two years in marketing to understand the function's importance to results. You know it in your bones, or through astute observation. Nor does a wildly creative type in marketing need to slog through a couple of years in operations to know that quality matters. Please. Yet, because of the received wisdom about "rounding yourself out," we've seen too many terrific functional experts jump out of their areas, only to vanish into the organizational ether.

Look, if you're really talented at something and you intentionally up and move yourself to an area where you're not so talented, it's like an ice hockey star quitting to join the NBA. (Or like Michael Jordan deciding to become a professional baseball player; we all remember where that went.) Our point is, don't wear skates to a basketball game. It's a surefire way to stall a career. And if you're finding that out for yourself right now, the fix is clear. Return to whence you belong. You'll soon be back in the game and your career will be too.

Then there are careers that stall because of an attitude problem. OK, that's being polite. We're talking about boss-haters. You know, the people who play by the rules outwardly, while inwardly they ooze disdain and disgust for the organization and its leaders.

The thing about boss-haters, we've realized after writing and talking about them for more than a decade, is that they rarely know they're boss-haters. *They* are not the problem, in their opinion. The company is the problem. The people in charge are fools and incompetents. They only care about money; they don't understand a thing about the customer or the products. And frankly, most of their coworkers aren't much better. They all suck up to the bigs and don't know anything useful.

As we said, we don't expect boss-haters to self-identify. But on the off chance these sentiments ring a bell, welcome to understanding why your career has stalled. And welcome, too, to accepting that, without a serious change in mindset, you *are* truly stuck. Because even if you're smart and capable—and boss-haters tend to be—no higher-up is ever going to give a leg up to someone who scorns them. It's not happening.

But enough about boss-haters. Luckily, they're relatively few in number. Let's turn finally to the most common reason that careers stall. Performance.

Or more precisely, underperformance.

Now, underperformance doesn't mean you're not trying hard at work. You might very well be giving it your all. But the last place effort counted more than results was in elementary school. This is real life.

Here's the problem, though. In real life, too many underperformers don't know that they're underperforming. The reason, as we said in Chapter 9, is that too many managers out there don't tell their people where they stand. They're too busy. Or they think people should figure it out on their own. Or they're too "kind" for straight-up candor, or so they claim.

None of these reasons make sense. In fact, as we said earlier, we'd argue that obfuscation around performance is cruel and unfair. People deserve to know how they're doing at something they're doing eight or ten hours a day. Come on.

But, sadly, that's the way it is. If you're in purgatory at a growing company, and you're not being blocked, you're not wearing ice skates to a basketball game, and you're not a boss-hater, you can assume that in the eyes of the powers-that-be, you're just not good enough to be promoted.

You're not big enough.

Now, we're not talking about *big enough* in terms of personality. In fact, sometimes having a big personality can hurt you as you try to ascend the ladder. People can read your extroversion as arrogance, or take you as a know-it-all or blowhard. People with big personalities can make very big targets of themselves.

No, we're talking about *big enough* in terms of having the breadth and depth to handle the next job.

Breadth and depth.

Regardless of the specifics of your job, that combination is what your bosses are waiting to see.

1. Don't Deliver. Overdeliver.

Ask yourself this: How close do you come to meeting your boss's expectations every day or month or quarter? Do you hit your targets? Make your quotas? Fulfill your order books?

If so, that's too bad. It's not enough.

If you want to demonstrate breadth and depth, the first change you need to make is not just meeting expectations. You must exceed them. You must overdeliver results. That means with every assignment, you must redefine its parameters to make it bigger, more exciting, more relevant, and more *everything* to make your boss smarter and make his or her job easier.

Remember, when your boss asks you to do a piece of work, they usually already have a sense of the answer. And they're figuring that you'll confirm that answer for them with your analysis, providing details or numbers to make the case easier to present to their own boss. Or even if your boss doesn't have a sense of the answer to a specific query, they do have an idea in their head about how your assignment should turn out.

Overdelivering means taking the presumed thinking or idea in your boss's head and elevating it to a whole new level.

Consider the case of two bright college grads we know who both landed one-year, up-or-out internships at an executive search firm in Chicago. After training with a team for about three months, each was asked to compile a list of candidates for an open position at a client's company.

Our first associate, let's call him Tom, had been getting somewhat mixed signals about his future. His work so far, his manager told him, was in the B to B-plus range. Good, he knew, but not good enough to land a permanent spot.

The other associate, Cindy, had joined the firm with an Ivy League halo over her head. She was invited to a couple of special lunches with senior executives, many of whom were impressed by her innate intelligence. Still, her on-the-job output was meh—no better than a C-plus.

As the assignment due date approached, Tom could barely sleep. He didn't want to live in his parents' basement forever, but even more than that, he longed for the impact that came with a permanent position. That's when it dawned on him: his boss would be *satisfied* with the assigned list of candidates, but he'd be *thrilled* with a wider and deeper picture of the industry, and in particular, one that suggested where potential new business might be found.

And so Tom set about creating such a picture. He did extensive digging to come up with a list of superstar candidates for the client, annotating the list with his assessment of how likely each was to be interested, based on his client's growth rate, and other factors. But Tom's final report also included the org charts of six companies in the same industry, with an emphasis on the fastest-growing among them.

Cindy, meanwhile, searched some of the firm's old files, poked around LinkedIn, and called an industry analyst she knew from college. Her list basically screamed, "Going through the motions."

You know how the story ends. Cindy is working in another field. Tom was hired and is on his way; he even has two interns of his own now. The difference is, he figured out that getting ahead isn't about handing in your homework on time.

It's about defining the extra credit, and then acing it.

2. Volunteer for Hard Duty

Exceeding expectations is something you can strive for every day, but every now and again, you get the opportunity to show your breadth and depth by volunteering for, and nailing, a hard assignment.

A hard, high-visibility assignment, and in particular, the one that nobody else wants to touch. The initiative that only the boss likes. The joint venture everyone thinks is going to flop. The manufacturing plant with the yield problem, located someplace very out of the way. The big new client known for outsized demands and impossible deadlines.

Unfortunately, many people in career purgatory shy away

from such prospects. They figure, "Why pile a public failure on top of a precarious situation?"

That question makes sense, until you realize the upside of succeeding at a kryptonite assignment. It has the potential to rebrand you from follower to leader, from muddler to winner, from maybe to yes.

True, you might fail. That's not the end of the world; you'll be able to add a line of new skills and experience to your resume as you look around for your next job.

In the best-case scenario, though, the impact will be galvanizing. In fact, you'll wonder why you waited so long to place a big, exciting bet on yourself.

3. Acquire Followers the Hard Way

A third change you can make to break your career impasse is the acquisition of followers. You need to show the organization that people—peers and bosses alike—listen when you talk.

Luckily, if you've embraced the first change of overdelivering results, the acquisition of followers should come pretty automatically. People generally want to hear what their organization's biggest contributors are saying.

So speak up.

That is, *prepare* and speak up.

Remember the head of HR we talked about in Chapter 3? He worked at a midwestern refrigeration manufacturer, one that had recently been acquired by a private equity fund. This leader changed the game for his company when he discovered that the company's performance evaluation processes were not being linked closely enough to its operations, and he demonstrated his findings with a chart that everyone could grasp with one look.

Insights like his, the kind of insights that improve companies and jump-start careers, do not come on the fly. The HR head had started with a competitive mindset. He'd been thinking like a company leader, driven by the question, "Why aren't these projects moving faster?" Then he'd dug into the data; he'd spent days with it. He was searching for an OMG idea, and he'd found it. And not only did his best practice make him a hero in his own company, it put him in front of every CEO in the private equity portfolio.

But data is just one quarry for you to mine to build your arsenal of smart insights. Every industry has thought leaders to read, academic research to plow through. There are podcasts, books, lectures, blogs, massive open online courses (MOOCs). Never miss a day of the *Wall Street Journal*.

The world is awash in ideas. Swim in them. Not just occasionally. All the time. Seek out higher intelligence from every quarter, synthesize ideas you've harvested, augment them with your own thinking and analysis, and bring them to your organization in ways that are relevant.

And have opinions—on everything. That really matters. No one wants to listen to a robot. Should Microsoft have bought Nokia? Who's the better long-term bet, Facebook or Twitter? Are activist shareholders good or bad for the economy? We're talking about those kinds of industry-shaping topics. If a big merger has just occurred in your industry, know all the players involved and form a view on whether it was a good or bad idea. If a competitor is reported to be working on a new technology, chase down the specifics and figure out how big a threat you think it poses. Keep track of the major leaders in your field and follow them in the print media and online. Over time, you'll begin to get a sense of what they believe about the future and how right or wrong they tend to be. Share those insights with your team.

Remember, you're not sharing either your insights or opinions to show off your big brain. Like the HR leader with the game-changing chart, you're sharing them to contribute to your organization's success.

When you do, people will look up when you talk. And soon, when it comes to your career, they'll starting thinking "up," too.

4. Make Sure You're Tech-Current

The next change we're going to talk about is probably most relevant to the over-40 crowd. Make that over 35.

Actually, make that anyone who's decided to leave technology expertise to the "kids."

Big mistake. Not being tech-current is a surefire way to lose your seat at the table where any and all important organizational and strategic issues are being discussed. It's purgatory glue.

A few years ago, we were interviewing several advertising agencies to represent our online MBA program. Very early into the process, we observed that every meeting boiled down to a discussion about a few key tech acronyms, like CPM (cost per thousand), CPC (cost per click), and CVR (conversion rate). When we commented on this fact with a potential agency, one of the lone gray-hairs in the meeting smiled sardonically. "The geeks rule the world," he said.

They do indeed. While advertising still contains its moments of artistic inspiration—think of those amazing Super Bowl commercials—the industry is increasingly driven by science and data analysis in the form of A/B testing, conversion rate optimization, and attribution modeling, among other technical wizardry. The implications for those who entered advertising ten or 20 years ago—or even five—are massive. If you want to get ahead in advertising, you will only rise if you do so along with its relentless tide of technology innovation.

It's the same story in industry after industry. You must push yourself to learn what you don't know, even if the analytics you don't understand scare you. Otherwise, when the real conversations take place, your chair will be in the hallway, and pretty soon it could be on the sidewalk.

Take the story of an executive we've known for decades; we'll call her Linda here.

It was 2011. Linda, who was in her mid-fifties at the time, was running HR at a $500 million manufacturing company that sold its widgets through a staff of around 200 salespeople across the country. She loved her job; the management team was terrific, and unlike at so many previous places she'd worked, Linda felt the CEO truly valued HR's input in key decisions.

But Linda also felt a creeping concern. Recently, every senior management meeting had ended up being about information derived from the company's newly adopted CRM system. Broadly speaking, Linda had a sense of the system's benefits, but she could see that her colleagues were fluent in its nuances. More and more, it was clear, they knew about each salesperson's performance in ways she did not.

Then one day, Linda's lack of deep familiarity came home to roost. Poring over the data from a recent CRM report, her colleagues started discussing whether the head of sales for the Northeast region should be reassigned, or perhaps even let go. As far as Linda was concerned, based on years of traditional performance evaluations, this manager was a solid performer, well liked by his team and customers. The data, however, seemed to be showing he'd plateaued in finding new business long ago, and his team had, too. Further, the whole region was clearly the least successful in its rollout of the company's new product strategy.

The meeting left Linda panicked. On the one hand, she was relieved no one had asked her opinion on the matter. Her "data" was obviously outdated to the point of uselessness. On the other, not being asked was an omen—a bad one.

The next morning, Linda tracked down the company's head of marketing and arranged for a two-day tutorial in the new CRM system, one in-house and the other with the system's vendor. She also asked the marketing VP to walk her through a recent CRM report—the one that had been discussed at the meeting about the Northeast region sales manager—highlighting which data trends were the most closely linked to the company's strategic goals. The session lasted four long hours, with Linda probing the meaning of practically every figure on every page.

"I wanted to be completely fluent in the system," Linda told us. "I *needed* to be. I was right on the brink of not mattering anymore, of not being taken seriously."

Our point here obviously isn't about CRM systems, per se. It's about waking up every day wondering what you don't know about your industry's technology and thinking *it could kill you.* Linda could have stayed in her HR silo and concerned herself only with HR terms and issues she natively understood. But that's the same thing as waving a white flag in business today. Linda earned back her place at the table with other senior executives, and you will, too, by knowing that technology savvy isn't optional anymore.

5. Get Real About Mentors

Sometimes, of course, expanding your expertise (be it in technology or other skills) takes more than the kind of dogged curiosity Linda displayed. In fact, sometimes it involves going back to school, either to get an advanced degree, earn a certificate, or take a seminar on the side. We are huge fans of continuing education—especially, given the economy, if you are able take your classes while staying employed full- or part-time. These days, you just don't want to lose the momentum of your career's trajectory.

But if continuing education is not an option (and even if it is), there's still the fifth change we're going to suggest in order to jump-start your career. Treat everyone around you as a mentor.

There it is. The M-word. We almost hesitate to use it.

Because "mentoring" is a buzzword. Parents, aunts, uncles, career coaches, leadership pundits—everyone tells you the same thing. Find a VIP in your company, form a bond, then sit back as he or she advises and protects you as you soar through the heavens.

The problem is, such knight-in-shining-armor mentors are as rare as, well, knights in shining armor. They come around when (and only when) a young businessperson shows extraordinary promise and the personal chemistry is perfect besides. Larry Summers, for instance, was an important mentor to Sheryl Sandberg at the start of her career. They met when Larry was Sheryl's professor at Harvard, where she was a star student, to put it mildly; later he recruited her to work for him at the World Bank, and after that, at the Treasury Department. It's generally understood that Sheryl, with her enormous brainpower and savvy, contributed to Larry's success nearly as much as he did to hers.

So, yes, the kind of mentoring relationship your parents dream of for you . . . it can happen. But it is rare, rare, rare.

That's why our strong advice is, no matter where you are in your career, consider *every* person in your sphere to be a mentor— young, old, and in between, in your area of expertise and outside it. From this circle of mentors, observe best practices. If someone in your field is a great speaker, study what she's doing right and incorporate it into your own presentations. If another manager in your division consistently on-ramps new employees well, copy his techniques. If you have a colleague or superior who runs a great meeting, see that individual as a teacher and a guide.

Look, everyone knows something you don't. Everyone.

Find that something and grab it to make your work smarter and better. Come to work each day committed to finding a better way to do everything you do, from the mundane on up. And in time—not immediately, but eventually—your breadth and depth will be much enhanced for it.

And your career will, too.

6. Love Everyone

The final strategy we're going to suggest in order to break your career stall is the hardest. It's loving everyone.

Loving everyone is distinctly different from the mentoring mindset we just described. The mentoring mindset is about engaging with a community of colleagues in an effort to put their brains inside yours.

Loving everyone is not a brain thing. It's a heart thing.

Anthropologists would tell you that people have separated themselves into tribes since the dawn of time. We've gathered allies and eliminated enemies to protect our interests. We've engaged in gossip to know what's really going on. Basically, they would assert, it's human nature to gossip, criticize, whisper, trade info, join a clique, form a cabal, or otherwise engage in palace intrigue.

So what?

Just. Don't. Do. It.

We know that's hard! We plead guilty to almost all of the above charges. We've gossiped, criticized, whispered, and on and on. But this has done us no good, and that's because it doesn't do anyone any good.

So here's another approach—one that really works. To the best of your ability, refuse to talk about other people unless it's in positive terms. Refuse to join surreptitious coalitions. Refuse to backstab and politick. At first, people may be perplexed by your absence from the cabals. However, in time, people will come to see you for what you are: trustworthy. A person who's about doing the work, not manipulating the workplace.

A person who demonstrates integrity and leadership.

Qualities on the basis of which promotions are made.

Purgatory, Dante wrote, was a place to avoid at all costs.

If you're in a career stall, you get that.

Our goal here has been to describe getting *out* with six action steps we believe will help you demonstrate new and improved breadth and depth. Deploy all of these options, or pick a few and go gangbusters.

Because getting unstuck is a transformative thing. It reminds you why you went into business in the first place. To grow. To make a difference. To create a great life. To have fun.

None of those things happen when you feel as if you're standing still. So don't just deliver and hope for the best. Overdeliver and expect more. Volunteer for hard duty. The worst thing that could happen is you gain experience; the best is a whole new reputation. Acquire followers with smart insights and strong opinions; get heard. Don't leave tech knowledge to the kids or let it be a function of age—embrace it like you're a kid yourself. Consider everyone a mentor; fill your brain with theirs. And finally, hard though it may be, trade in politicking and nattering for kindness and encouragement.

Love has a way of going round and round.

13. IT AIN'T OVER TILL IT'S OVER

We end this book with a chapter about beginnings.

The facts are, few careers go exactly as planned. Few careers, at least that we know of, go straight up-up-uphill without hitting at least one bump in the road, and usually more. In other words, most of us change jobs at some point—once, twice, and maybe even several times over a 40- or 50-year run. Sometimes it's by our own volition, sometimes not. And, then, comes retirement. The grand finale.

Each one of these endings puts us at the starting line all over again.

How great.

Yes, we mean that. Starting over allows us to reinvent ourselves, to wipe the slate clean and paint a whole new masterpiece. What could be more exciting? Even when the circumstances are not of our choosing, reinvention is an opportunity to grow, and create a more fulfilling, abundant life. To see an ending any other way—with say, fear, dread, or loathing—yes, that's human, but negativity is always self-defeating. It eats us alive.

Recently one of us spoke at Cornell University to a group of women business school students. The topic of the speech was, "What I Wish I Knew at 21." Item 1 was: You cannot fail.

That's right: *You cannot fail.* Sure, we said, you can royally screw up. You can run a project that flops. You can hire a dolt who wrecks your team's karma. You can get asked to pack up your desk and go home. You can retire and wake up one morning to find you're lost, and tired, bored out of your mind. No matter. It's only over if it's over in your head.

Don't ever let it be. Every ending is just an opportunity to start again, wiser, more experienced, and more emboldened for the next act.

The "you cannot fail" message was, we could tell, a bit of a shock to the Cornell audience. The world as they've experienced it—as we all sometimes experience it—can feel like one big rejection machine, waiting to spit you out.

There is no machine. There's only life. And it ain't over till it's over, and we mean *really* over.

Until then, when an ending happens, you have the choice to cower, or freak out, or do nothing—or embrace an ending for what it can be.

An invitation to make yourself anew.

TO HELL AND BACK

That invitation generally presents itself in three career situations. Let's start with the worst of them: being let go.

OK, "let go" is a bit of a euphemism. In your own mind, even if you can't say the words out loud, you've been fired. And even though getting fired is more prevalent now than it's ever been, it has to be one of the most painful experiences you'll endure in your life, replete with sadness, embarrassment, and anger.

It can paralyze us. "I have nowhere to go," we think. "It's over."

Take the story of Graham.

For nearly 15 years, Graham was a senior PR executive at a regional branding and communications firm, until one morning in 2010, he wasn't anymore.

"I'm in shock," he kept repeating when he called us with the news of his layoff. "How could this happen to me?"

The answer to that question was actually pretty simple. Graham wasn't an underperformer—he was in the top 40 percent of his firm—but his salary was a big, fat problem. With his long tenure, it was probably 35 percent higher than a good replacement might cost, and the replacement would likely be more aggressive about generating new business. When the economy softened, that made Graham a prime target for goodbye.

Regardless, he hadn't seen it coming. And his response— along with the disbelief—played out as you might expect. "I'm never leaving my house again," he told us, not completely joking. "Everyone in the city knows I got canned."

Look, as we've said, it's only human to reel for a while after you've been let go. Indeed, you might even reel until you're on your knees. But we're in the tough-love school on this matter. Mourn, cry, rage—fine. But then, you have to summon the courage and fortitude to end the pity party. End it before you want to. Because, like a smart lady at our church once said, "The problem with a pity party is that, after a while, you notice you're the only one there."

Without doubt, there are various ways to "get over" being fired so that you can get on with your reinvention. Counseling, friendship, family, exercise, prayer, meditation, or perhaps just a good old-fashioned "Snap out of it!" moment. But in our experience, you can't really move on from your firing until you own it.

That's right, own it. You need to understand why you were let go, and accept responsibility for your part in it. If you recall, in Chapter 2, we talked about the power of owning a competitive whack, such as a botched product rollout. Same thing here, only this time, it's personal.

Now, we understand that it's only natural to want to blame someone or something else for your situation. A jerk boss. A conniving coworker. The crummy economy. But blame, like its cousin, negativity, is an emotion that keeps us in the same place. It keeps us from framing our firing as a learning experience, and a jumping-off point for us, only in a new-and-improved incarnation.

So do it. Come up with an ownership statement. "I was let go because I missed one too many deadlines and my boss lost confidence in me." Or: "I was fired because I never really believed in the product and that attitude showed itself in too many ways, large and small." Or: "I hit my numbers every quarter, but I guess I never got totally comfortable with sharing ideas."

Even if your firing was not entirely of your own making, own every part that was.

Eventually Graham did just that. "The economy nailed my whole industry, and we weren't immune. But I thought my tenure would protect me. I was clueless—I should have been thinking about the whole company, thinking like the CEO," he said. "The truth was my tenure made me the perfect cost to cut because I wasn't generating the new business we needed. I wasn't earning my keep."

Owning your ending is like a cold reality shower. Invigorating.

And empowering. It galvanizes you to correct—and even overcorrect—the error of your ways as you go forward again. It makes you savvier, more self-aware, and just plain better.

If ho-hum was Graham's weakness in the past, you would never know it now. After his noncompete expired, he started his own firm, and today he pursues clients with a fierceness that makes you think of the phrase "hungry like a wolf." He billed $1.5 million last year, and just expanded to a second city.

That would have never happened if he'd let his firing define him. Instead, he defined it, as a brand-new chapter, with himself as the author.

A NEW UNIFORM

The second situation in our careers that invites reinventions occurs when we change companies.

Huh?

Why, you might be wondering, would you reinvent yourself when that happens? If you've been hired by a new place, surely you've already got the right stuff. And if you've been kept on during an acquisition, again, you must be OK.

True and true. But here's the thing: Joining a new organization, whether you've been hired or acquired, is like becoming a citizen of another country. You may have sung the national anthem as your plane touched down on foreign soil, but you have piles and piles to learn before you can call yourself a native. A new language, new customs, new people, new processes and practices. New subtleties in the culture you cannot even see yet.

So do yourself a favor and let go of the notion that you can think and act the same way as you always have. And consider the possibility—and perhaps even embrace the possibility—that you can learn and grow, if you'd only let down your defenses and be wide open to change.

No, we're not suggesting you toss out your authentic self, or your personal values, or the valuable knowledge you've accumulated over the years. That would be nonsense. Rather, we're suggesting you take your "citizenship" of the new company as an opportunity to augment and expand your repertoire of skills, try on new behaviors, and shake up your assumptions about how everything should get done.

Consider the case of an executive we met when he attended one of our two-day seminars on leadership. The man had spent nearly his whole career at a family-owned firm in the California wine business. In fact, he was head of sales, managing a team of

100 reps, when it was acquired by a European conglomerate. On one hand, the acquisition was great news for the executive, as the new owner was promising to pour significant new resources into marketing. On the other hand, the new owner had also installed a management team of Europeans, who were, in our executive's estimation, rather grim and unappealing. They killed the routine pre-meeting conversation about sports, downsized the popular company lunchroom, and demanded an approach to customer service that struck many of the "old-timers" as cold and impersonal.

A career disaster in the making?

Actually, no, because the executive in this situation decided he'd rather reinvent himself than quit. He loved Napa, believed in his company's product, and he sensed that the acquirer might actually be able to create a great future for himself and the whole organization. And so, he put away his "That's not the way we used to do it" attitude and set about learning the "why" behind every new practice. In meetings and private conversations alike, he gently probed with questions like, "Can you help me understand the thinking behind our new forecasting method?" and, "Could you walk me through how you came to that assessment of the midwestern market, because it's new and very exciting to me?" The executive, in other words, signaled he was eager to join the program, and he'd invest the energy and demonstrate the open-mindedness to do so.

It's a winning reaction to encountering the new—saying "Wow," instead of "Whoa." Sure, your old ways and strengths may have suited you fine. But that was at your old place.

Build on that foundation. Just know your new place beckons a new you—open to change, from the inside out.

AFTER THE GOODBYE PARTY

And now, retirement.

For most of us, retirement is the exact opposite experience of being let go; it's goodbye with tears of joy.

Goodbye to the routine. Goodbye to the meetings and more meetings. Goodbye to people controlling your schedule. Goodbye to the manufacturing plants and their relentless drumbeat of productivity demands. Goodbye to the same old sales calls. Goodbye to charging your phone while sitting on the floor of the airport terminal while waiting for your plane, which has been delayed in Chicago.

You finally own your own time.

Sometimes retirement also brings a kind of intellectual relief. A time can come when you're out of fresh ideas and you have nothing left to add to the business you're in. Perhaps you passed the regular retirement age and looked around only to notice that you'd become a blocker, holding back the younger people in your organization who were waiting for you to finally leave so they could have the careers they'd been longing for. You had a responsibility to those people and you knew it.

So, go in peace.

Just don't retire.

Reinvent.

Say goodbye—and then say hello. To something new. Something meaningful. Something big.

If you never worked in your Area of Destiny, retirement is the time to start. Go back to school; learn what you need to. Find a new activity and create the kind of life you've always wanted to live.

Start a business, like our friend Graham. It can be on your old familiar ground, or in a totally new field. Buy a franchise. Become a partner at a start-up that could use someone with your decades of know-how. Throw yourself into volunteering for a cause that makes your heart do somersaults.

Just don't stop growing.

Play some golf. Plant a garden. Travel the country or the world. Write a novel. All those activities you waited for. Just avoid stasis like the plague. Stasis is what causes too many retired people to sit around pining for the old days, feasting on nostalgia for a time that never was.

That helps no one; let it go.

Let yourself and your energy go—someplace altogether different. Retirement allows you—heck, it practically begs you—to live in the past. Reinvention spurs you to live in the present and future.

Technically, we both retired in 2001. (OK, one of us retired; the other got fired for running off with the one of us who retired.) Ahead of us, all we saw was uncharted territory, crying out for exploration. And explore we did, especially with the launch of our online MBA program. We became entrepreneurs! That's what reinvention's all about. Haven't-been-there, haven't-done-that.

Obviously, we're not unique in our retirement reboot. Not by any measure. We all know lots and lots of stories of people with deeply fulfilling "second careers." Andy Pearson of PepsiCo, Bill

George of Medtronic, and Kevin Sharer of Amgen all retired from corporate America and became professors at Harvard Business School. Cal Ripken Jr., the baseball great who retired in 2001 after 21 seasons with the Baltimore Orioles, launched a business comprising two youth-oriented sports complexes, speaking engagements, and television broadcasting. He also owns two minor-league teams. You get the sense that for Cal Jr., a legend when he retired at age 40, a new story is just beginning.

Such reinventions are hardly the purview of CEOs and sports stars. We recently met an entrepreneur in the insurance industry who sold his company, retired, and then went back to school to become a physical therapist. He now works at New York's Hospital for Special Surgery and has never been happier. We know a retired New York City police officer who built a successful career as an owner's representative, overseeing complicated construction projects. A retired plant pathologist who started a coffee farm in Honduras. A retired medical industry executive who entered divinity school. A retired IT director who became a jazz musician.

We could go on and on, but here's the point: when a career ends, life does not.

It only means a new life can begin.

OK, we'll admit it, some things do end.

This chapter about the excitement of reinvention, for one.

And this book for another.

Together, we've covered a lot of ground since we set out with the goal of making *The Real-Life MBA* your partner as you play the greatest game on earth, business. No one, we said, should do business alone. It is the ultimate team sport, and thanks again for letting us be on your team.

To that end, we've served up just about everything we know about competition and strategy, globalization and growth, finance and marketing. We've laid out our best thinking on leading with truth-seeking and trust-building as your beacons, creating a wow team, and managing the "geniuses, tramps, and thieves" that can make work, well, particularly interesting. Finally, we've gotten into the trenches of your career, helping you figure out, we hope, what you should make of it, how to advance it, and how to make sure it never really ends.

Because work is great. It's life. It's what we do.

Every day better.

ACKNOWLEDGMENTS

We make the case in this book that business is a team sport. Well, so is writing a book. Thank goodness we've been able to take the field over the past decade with so many great people. Smart, wise, bold, generous, creative. People just filled with stuff. For the many ways you helped us forge the concepts and practices in this book, we love you and we thank you.

First, there are the leaders and entrepreneurs of businesses large and small whose stories and insights fill the pages you've just read: Dave Calhoun, Erik Fyrwald, Joe DeAngelo, Michael Petras, Dennis Gipson, Scott Mannis, Vindi Banga, Paul Pressler, Bunny Williams, Joey Levin, Michael Zeliff, Susan Jacobson, and Griff Long. Each one of you is a beacon of intelligence, and we know your experiences will serve as valuable guidance to your fellow travelers on the long, winding, and occasionally bumpy road to business success. Our ample gratitude, too, to the contributors to this book, who, for various understandable reasons, asked that their real or full names not appear with their stories.

Over the past decade-plus, we've also been surrounded by people who have just plain made us smarter—much, much smarter—by dint of their words and actions. Don Gogel, of the private equity firm Clayton Dubilier & Rice, has been a great teacher about PE industry dynamics and deal-making, all while demonstrating a perfect touch in the complex art of managing a partnership. Barry Diller, founder and CEO of IAC, has been a terrific business partner, whose incisive mind, energy, and competitive courage has taught us oceans about entrepreneurship and the online space. Bill Conaty, coauthor of *The Talent Masters: Why Smart Leaders Put People Before Numbers*, ran HR at GE for two decades, and has remained a close friend and business associate ever since. His deep knowledge about people management, shared in countless conversations, infuses our own thinking, and thus countless passages in *The Real-Life MBA*.

Many of the stories and ideas in this book sprang from robust conversations with the faculty, staff, and students of the Jack Welch Management Institute at Strayer University. We are grateful to JWMI's dean, Dr. Andrea Backman, and its CEO, Dean Sippel, for building JWMI into the exciting institution it's become, and to Strayer's executive chairman, Rob Silberman, and its CEO, Karl McDonnell, for their steadfast support in that process.

We first heard the term "Area of Destiny" when Terry E.

Smith, pastor of the Life Christian Church in Orange, N.J., and author of *10: How Would You Rate Your Life?*, spoke at our own church one Sunday morning. We thank you, Terry, for so graciously allowing us to borrow and adapt your concept to a business context.

And then there's Hollis Heimbouch of HarperBusiness, publisher *extraordinaire*. Hollis shepherded this book from a few scrawled notes on the back of a paper napkin to its completed form, and did so with grace, humor, and editorial virtuosity. She's the best in the biz. Speaking of superlatives, Bob Barnett of Williams & Connolly, was integral to the launching of this book, and we are grateful for that (once again).

We also received masterful editorial polishing from Megan Slatoff-Burke, JWMI's director of marketing, whose razor-sharp intelligence simply made this book better.

Every team needs a cheering section, and we were blessed to have a great one in the form of our wonderful blended family. Thank you all for loving us through our bouts of whining, moaning, and complaining, and for celebrating with us when it was done.

Finally, this book would not have been possible without the forbearance and flat-out help of Rosanne Badowski. Rosanne joined the Welch team (as Jack's assistant) in 1988. Yes, 1988. And, yes, she's still making the whole thing work. Thank you, Rosie Ro. We promise, no more books.

At least not for a few more years.

INDEX

A

acquisitions, 132, 133

actionable data, 31, 56–57

advertising

    advertorials, 134–35

    consumers' ad blindness, 92

    and technology, 207

alignment

    about, 3–5, 14, 22

    anonymous employee survey on, 78–79

    behaviors and mission, 8–12

    consequences related to, 4, 12–14

    grind/gridlock vs., 2–3, 22

    and hiring checklists, 143–44, 145–47

    See also behaviors; mission

alignment tactics

    about, 15

    communicate the mission and behaviors, constantly, 17–18, 124

    make work fun, 21–22, 125, 149–50

    practice generosity with words and deeds, 19–20, 30, 124, 139, 149

    provide coach-like support for your employees, 16–17, 130–31 remove blockages from your people's way, 18–19, 58–59, 124

Amazon.com, 108–9

Angelou, Maya, 116

anonymous survey of employees, 78–79

AOD (Area of Destiny) career assessment process

about, 179–81, 192

identifying opportunities that fit you, 183–85

identifying what you love to do, 182–83

identifying what you're good at, 181–82

making the shift, 185

in retirement, 221

success stories, 179, 183–86

Area of Destiny. See AOD

arrogance, 147

aspirational mission, 6–7

assets, 82

AssuraMed, 46–48, 49–50, 55, 56–57, 60

attitude problems/boss haters, 199–200

auctions, online, and B2B marketing, 106–7

audiovisual design and installation company, 162–63

B

B2B marketing (business-to-business)

about, 105–6, 110

and Amazon.com, 108–9

analyzing industry capacity and capability, 107–8

foreign competition, RFPs, and online auctions, 106–7

personal relationships, 106, 107, 108

B2C marketing (business-to-consumer)

about, 110

and big data, 30–31

market research company, 5–7, 10, 12–13, 144–45

and products, 93–95, 110

See also Five Ps of marketing

balance sheet, 81–82

Banga, Vindi, 65–66, 71

Bates Motel (TV program), 103

Baumgartner, Felix, 102

behaviors

about, xi, 4

after whacking, 27

alignment with mission, 8–12, 124

budgeting-related, 129–30

communicating about, constantly, 17–18

gossip, 135–36, 146, 172, 211

at market research company, 10, 144

and role model management tool, 135, 150

values vs., 9

at water quality company, 10–12

Berges, Jim, 106, 107, 108

big data, 30–31, 56–57, 205

blockages, removing, 18–19, 58–59, 124

blockers and career-stall, 197–98

bonuses. See rewards

boss haters, 199–200

bribery in foreign markets, 70–71

budgeting and truth-seeking, 129–30

Bunny Williams Home, 71–72, 73, 189

bureaucracy in organizations, 18–19, 22, 124, 156

business

constant changes, viii, ix–x

crisis survival by most, 114

insularity in, 103–4

performance drivers, 30–32

social architecture reality-check, 36–38

sports equated to, vii–viii, 2, 16

today's challenges, ix

See also health of a business

business culture

and action blockers or change resisters, 19, 58–59

bureaucracies, 18–19, 22, 124, 156

and crises, 113–19, 132

and employee retention, 149–51, 155

fun as part of, 21–22, 125, 149–50

information lockdown, 132

and role model management tool, 135, 150

silos, 103–4

socialization of telecommuters, 164, 165, 167–68

wow environment, 149–51

See also rewards; teambuilding

business-to-business. *See* B2B marketing

business-to-consumer. *See* B2C marketing

C

Calhoun, Dave, 6–7, 10, 12–13, 144–45

career management

about, xii, 192–93, 213–14

choosing a career, 180

entrepreneurism, 186–90, 192

loving your job, 179

staying in a get-me-out-of-here job, 177–78

work-life choice, 190–92, 193

See also AOD career assessment process; career-stall solutions

career-stall

about, 195–96, 212

attitude problems/boss haters, 199–200

blockers, 197–98

multifunctional expertise myth, 198–99

underperformance, 200–201

career-stall solutions

about, 212

acquire followers, 204–6

be tech-current, 206–9

love everyone, 211–12

mentors, 209–10

overdeliver, 201–3

time limit for tolerating a blocker situation, 197, 198

volunteer for hard duty, 203–4

cash flow, 78, 80

championship project during whack recovery, 28

change

constant changes in business, viii, ix–x

and crisis management, 113–14

with role model management, 135, 150

technology and marketing, 91–92

Chief Meaning Officer, 17–18, 124

China, 11, 63–64

Clinton, Bill, 145

coach-like support for your employees, 16–17, 130–31

communication

as crisis management preparation, 115–18

of mission and behaviors, 17–18, 124

compensation, 56–57

competitors and competition

assessment of, 33–34, 206

competitive chain reaction, 107–8

and profitability, 96, 97

compliance for managing global risk, 70

conflict-creators, 170–71

consequences, 4, 12–14

consulting, viii, ix, 3

consumer brand and crisis management, 116–17

consumers

evolution of, 92–93, 96

price sensitivity, 97

responding to needs of, 73

See also B2C marketing

continuing education, 209

contract workers or freelancers (tramps), 158, 163–68, 173

Coolidge, Calvin, ix

crisis management

developing a robust public voice before the crisis, 115–18

goodwill stockpile for, 115–16

knowing it will pass, 118–19

listening during, 132–33

original principles, 113–14

personal crises, 116, 117

and social media, 112, 114–15, 117

CRM (customer relations management) program, 165–66, 207–9

culture. See business culture

curling metaphor, 18, 58

customer satisfaction, 79, 86

D

Dante, 195, 196, 212

data, big, 30–31, 56–57, 205

David's Bridal, 64–65, 70

DeAngelo, Joe, 26–27, 28–29, 31, 40, 44

details in foreign markets, 71–72

diagnostics in whack recovery process, 30–31

differentiation, 151–53, 154–55, 166–67

digital testing, 100

discernment as most needed quality abroad, 62, 67–69, 144

Disney, 68–69

drama-seekers, 146

E

emotionality of employees, 146

empathy in negotiations, 137

employees

about, xii

action blockers and change resisters, 19, 58–59

changing companies, 217–20

conflict-creators, 170–71

and dinner with the boss, 53

drama-seekers, 146

emotionality of, 146

employee engagement indicator of business health, 78–79

energizing with growth, 60

geniuses, xii, 101, 158, 159–63, 173

inspiring with generosity, 19–20, 30, 124, 139, 149

integrity violations, 158

leaving the job, 196

listening to, 132–33

and NPS customer satisfaction measurement system, 79

pay rates and bonuses, 148–49

performance appraisal and reward system, 13–14

productivity drains, 158–59

retaining the best in whack recovery process, 29–30

underperformers, 158–59, 168–70

unpleasant people as, 146

See also firing employees; performance appraisal system; teambuilding

entrepreneurism, 186–90, 192

entrepreneurs, 188

Equinox, 179

European conglomerate in Napa Valley wine business, 218–19

experiential marketing, 101–3

experimentation without attachment marketing, 99–101

experimentation with surprise marketing, 101–3

export strategies, 62–64

F

Facebook, 61

facilitating gratuity/payments, 70–71

faculty rating system at JWMI, 166–67

failure, impossibility of, 214

fear as a thief, 159, 171–73

finance

about, xi, 75–76, 80–81, 89

administrative HR as part of, 154

assets, 82

balance sheet, 81–82

budgeting and truth-seeking, 129–30

and business health indicators, 77–81

cash flow, 78, 80

income statement, 82–84

liabilities, 82

marketing cost analysis, 87–88

P&L statement, 80, 83–84

shareholder equity, 82

and truth-seeking questions, 160–61

variance analysis, 77, 84–86, 87–89

firing employees

as alignment consequence, 12–13

crises resulting from, 117–18

differentiation process, 152

leaders owning responsibility for, 138, 139

trust-building methods, 137–39

underperformers, 169–70

Five Ps of marketing

about, 93–94

people, 103–5

place, 95–97

price, 97–99

product, 94–95

promotion, 99–103

Five Slides strategy process, 32–34, 128

focus groups, 100

focusing on one or two growth initiatives, 49–51

followers, acquiring, 204–6, 212

foreign markets. *See* globalization

Four Es and a P framework, 125

"Four Reasons to Quit Your Job" (Welch and Welch), 177–78

freelancers or contract workers (tramps), 158, 163–68, 173

fresh eyes results, 46–48

fun at work, 21–22, 125, 149–50

Fyrwald, Erik, 7–8, 10, 12, 13

G

General Motors, 38

generosity gene, 19–20, 30, 124, 139, 149

geniuses, xii, 101, 158, 159–63, 173

getting in everyone's skin, 15–17, 124

Gibbs, Kristin, 48

Gipson, Dennis, 54

global best practice, 70

global brands, 63

globalization

about, 61–62, 74

and B2B marketing, 106–10

discernment as most needed quality abroad, 62, 67–69, 144

expanding into nearby markets, 72–74

exporting strategies, 62–64

risk level reality, 69–72

sourcing, 64–65

win-win positions, 62–66

good judgment in foreign markets, 68–69

goodwill and crisis management, 115–16

gossip, 135–36, 146, 172, 211

grind/gridlock, 2–3, 22

grind, overcoming, 3–5, 15. *See also* alignment

growth

about, 43–45, 59–60

AssuraMed story, 46–48, 49–50, 55, 56–57, 60

concentrating effort on one or two initiatives, 49–51

and customer service, 79

fresh eyes results, 46–48

growth mindset, 44–45

hunger for, 11

and innovation mindset, 51–53

matching talent to the task, 53–55, 204–5

obstacle removal, 58–59

and opportunities for upward mobility, 197

order rate increases, 85–86

results of traditional efforts, 47

rewards for, 56–57

stagnation in, 44

See also alignment; whack-recovery tactics

growth resisters, 19, 58–59

"Gypsies, Tramps, and Thieves" (Cher), 157

H

happiness and employee retention, 148

HD Supply (HDS), 26–27, 31, 35–36, 40

health of a business

about, 77–78

and cash flow, 78, 80

and crisis management ability, 115–19

and customer satisfaction, 79, 86

employee engagement indicator, 78–79

Hertz Connect, 178–79

hiring checklists, 143–44, 145–47

hiring employees, 142–47

home health care products company, 46–48, 49–50

Hong Kong, 68–69

HR (human resources)

administrative, 154

bad rap, 153–54

new construct for, 154–55

truth-seeking questions for, 128

human nature vs. loving everyone, 211–12

Hussmann, 54–55, 204–5

I

IBM, 102

ideas

and entrepreneurism, 187–89, 192

and preparing for a promotion, 205

income statement, 82–84

Inferno (Dante), 195, 196, 212

innovation

about, ix, xi

as everyone's job, 45, 51–53

experimentation with surprise marketing as, 101–3

and foreign markets, 73

as growth driver, 51

as incremental improvements, 52, 53

as mindset, 52–53

inspirational mission, 6–7

insularity in business, 103–4

intangible assets, 82

integration, passion for, 10

integrity

about, 211–12

boosting trust of employees, 139

celebrating ownership/credit where it's due, 131–32

on hiring checklist, 143

same story for everyone as, 137

saying no to bribery, 70–71

values that promote, 115

violations of, 139, 158

internships, 202–3

IT function, importance of, 36, 37–38

It's Everybody's Business (online series), 178

J

Jack Welch Management Institute (JWMI) MBA program, ix, 79, 164–67, 206–7

Jacobson Strategic Communications, 167–68

Jacobson, Sue, 167–68

Jacobs, Paul, 35

Japan, 63, 64, 68

journalists and crisis management, 113

JPMorgan Chase, 38

JWMI (Jack Welch Management Institute) MBA program, ix, 79, 164–67, 206–7

K

Knauss, Don, 16–17

Korea, 64

L

Land, Edwin, 110

Las Vegas, Nevada, 1–2

leaders

    caring like crazy for their people, 16–17, 130–31

    changing companies, 217–20

    and claiming (or not) of credit, 131–32

    communicating the mission and behaviors, constantly, 17–18, 124

    Four Es and a P framework, 125

    and generosity gene, 19–20, 30, 124, 139, 149

    listening, 132–33

    making work fun, 21–22, 125, 149–50

    managing fear, 171–73

    and multiple constituencies, 136–37

    owning responsibility for firing employees, 138, 139

    removing blockages, 18–19, 58–59, 124

    role model management, 135, 150

    talking to subordinates about each other, 135–36

    what-if-ers and worst-casers, 32–33

    See also managers

leadership

    about, 123–25, 139–40

    and alignment of behaviors with mission, 9, 22

    and CIO, 37

    See also truth-and-trust leadership

Leahy, Sir Terry, 31

learning, viii, ix, x–xi

Levin, Joey, 159–61

Lewinsky, Monica, 112

liabilities, 82

listening, 132–33

location and marketing, 95–97

Long, Griff, 178–79, 183

loving everyone, 211–12

M

managers

    communicating mission and behaviors, 18

    customer visits, 79

and foreign assignments, 67

hiring mistakes, 142–43

milquetoast managers, 16

pompous and self-important managers, 15–16

retaining the best in whack recovery process, 29–30

sucking the fun out vs. filling souls, 21–22, 150

and underperformers, 168–70

See also leaders

Mannis, Scott, 54–55, 204–5

manufacturing companies, 54–55, 127, 204–5

Marine Corps mess allegory, 16–17

marketing

about, xi, 93

and consumer evolution, 92–93, 96

cost analysis, 87–88

creative genius model, 101

fresh eyes results, 48

technology and changes to, 91–92

See also B2B marketing; B2C marketing; Five Ps of marketing

market research company, 5–7, 10, 12–13, 144–45

markets

analysis/reviews, 33, 34–35

and globalization, 72–74

moving and changing, 32

market share and ROI variance analysis, 86

Mayer, Marissa, 163

MBA program, online, ix, 79, 164–67, 206–7

McCarthy, E. Jerome, 93. *See also* Five Ps of marketing

media and crisis management, 113, 114

mentors, 209–10, 212

meritocracies, 153

messaging (promotion), 99–103

"me-want" and marketing, 94–95

Miller's Pabst Blue Ribbon in China, 63

mindset

boss hater, 199–200

everyone is a mentor, 209–10

growth as, 44–45

innovation as, 52–53

loving everyone, 211–12

"make a killing" in foreign markets, 62

what-if-ers and worst-casers, 32–33

See also alignment; truth-and-trust leadership

Mindspark, 159–60

mission

about, xi, 4

aligning behaviors with, 8–12, 124

aspirational, inspirational, and practical, 6–7

communicating about, constantly, 17–18

and employees, 7

employees focused and fired up by, 8

and hiring process, 143–44, 145

in whack recovery, 28

See also alignment

MIT's Sloan School, 187

momentum and life direction, 180.

See also AOD career assessment process

multifunctional expertise and career-stall, 198–99

N

Nalco, 7–8, 10–12, 13

native advertising, 134–35

natural disasters, 24

negative energy in job applicant, 146

negotiations, 137

Neiman Marcus, 102

Nestlé's Kit Kat in Japan, 63

net income, 80, 85

Net Promoter Score (NPS), 79

New York Times, 111

Nielsen, 6–7, 10, 12–13, 144–45

NPS (Net Promoter Score), 79

O

oil and gas unit of water quality company, 11–12

online auctions and B2B marketing, 106–7

online sales, 96

openness behavior, 10

operating rate and working capital turnover ratio variance analysis, 86

operations, xi

opinions on industry-shaping topics, 205–6

order rate increases, 85–86

orders and salaried employment variance analysis, 85

Oreo, 104–5

organization chart, 36–38

overdelivering, 201–3, 212

ownership statement when fired, 216–17

P

Pabst Blue Ribbon in China, 63

Page, Larry, 25

paralyzer (fear), 159, 171–73

Paris metaphor for finance, 76

passion, 10, 11, 17–18

PE. *See* private equity firms

performance appraisal system
differentiation, 151–53, 154–55, 166–67

and growth initiatives, 54–55

lack of, 126–27, 200

and letting someone go, 138

and rewards, 13–14, 56–57

See also rewards

performance-based pay rates, 148

performance drivers in whack recovery process, 30–32

personal crises, 116, 117

Petras, Michael, 46–47, 48, 49–50, 55, 60

place and marketing, 95–97

Plank, Kevin, 114

P&L statement, 80, 83–84

Polaroid, 110

practical mission, 6–7

Pressler, Paul, 64–65, 68–69, 70

price and marketing, 97–99

price testing, 98

private equity (PE) firms

and AssuraMed, 46

budgeting behavior, 129

and details of how business was run, 127

mission-making examples, 5–8, 22

productive worry, 38–40

products

and consumer marketing, 93–95, 110

fragrance designer, 83–84

recommendations from peers, 92–93

profitability, 82–84, 96, 97

promotion and marketing, 99–103

promotions. *See* rewards

pull in marketing, 95

push in marketing, 95

R

raises. *See* rewards

rating system for faculty at JWMI, 166–67

reality-check of social architecture, 36–38

RealReal, 98

recognition. *See* rewards

Red Bull, 102

reference-checking in hiring process, 147

refrigeration manufacturing business, 54–55, 204–5

reinventing yourself

about, 213–14

changing companies, 217–20

failure not an option, 214

fired from a job, 215–17

retirement, 220–22

See also AOD career assessment process

requests for proposals (RFPs), 106, 107

resource allocation and growth, 49–51

responsibility for being fired, 216–17

retirement, 220–22

return on investment (ROI) and market share variance analysis, 86

rewards (promotions, raises, bonuses, and recognition)

as consequence, 13–14

for incremental innovations, 53

and leader's generosity gene, 19–20, 30, 124, 139, 149

pay rates and bonuses, 148–49

performance-based, 56–57

reexamining and refreshing the system, 56–57

utilizing for growth resisters, 59

in whack recovery process, 28, 29–30

See also performance appraisal system

RGH Enterprises. *See* AssuraMed

rigor

applied to truth-seeking, 128, 134–35

in hiring process, 145

risk management, importance of, 36–38

risk of operating in foreign markets, 69–72

ROI (return on investment) and market share variance analysis, 86

role model management, 135, 150

Roman Coliseum–like world metaphor, 111, 112

Roosevelt, Franklin, 172–73

S

salaried employment variance analysis, 85, 86

sales and net income variance analysis, 85

sales department and growth initiatives, 56–57

sales, online, 98

Sandberg, Sheryl, 210

secrets, 113

self-confidence, 147

SG&A (selling, general, and administrative) expenses, 88

shareholder equity, 82

silos, 103–4

simplicity behavior, 10

social architecture reality-check, 36–38

socialization of telecommuters, 164, 165, 166–68

social media

    and crisis management, 112, 114–15, 117

    Facebook, 61

    product recommendations from peers, 92–93

    public voice as crisis management preparation, 116–17

    Twitter, 102, 104–5, 112

    utilizing for spur-of-the-moment ad campaign, 104–5

software development company, 159–60

Sony, 38

sourcing, 64–65, 70, 73

sports and business equated, 2, 16

Sri Lanka, 64–65, 70

stalled careers. See career-stall

Stanford University, 187

starting over. See reinventing yourself

strategy

    cross-department agility, 104–5

    employee survey on, 78–79

    exporting strategies, 62–64

    Five Slides process, 32–34, 128

    and price, 98

    process reinvention, 32, 34–36

    silos vs., 103–4

    as truth finding exercise, 127–28

"Stratos Mission to transcend human limits" (Red Bull marketing ploy), 102

Suits (TV program), 103

Summers, Larry, 210

survey of employees, anonymous, 78–79

T

Taco Bell, 117

Target, 37

teambuilding

    about, xii, 141–42, 156

    and differentiation, 151–53, 154–55

    employee retention, 148–51, 155

    hiring process, 142–47

    and HR, 154–55

    and "wow" work environment, 149–51

technology
  being tech-current, 206–9, 212
  and IT function, 36, 37–38
  and marketing, 91–92
  whacks in tech businesses, 24
  working with techies, 159–63
telecommuters
  about, xii, 163–64, 173
  monitoring work, 166
  socialization of, 164, 165, 166–68
thieves
  about, 158–59, 173
  conflict-creators, 170–71
  fear, 159, 171–73
  underperformers, 158–59, 168–70
Thoreau, Henry David, 21
time limit for a blocker situation, 197, 198
tramps (freelancers or contract workers), 158, 163–68, 173
trust-building in real time
  keeping confidences and fairness, 135–36
  and letting people go, 137–39
  by loving everyone, 211–12
  in meetings, 133–35
  and negotiations, 137
  telling the same story to everyone, 136–37
trust dividend, 130–33
truth-and-trust leadership
  about, xi–xii, 15, 123, 125, 140
  for creating a "wow" workplace, 150

  and differentiation, 151–53, 154–55, 166–67
  no mysteries about the work, 160
  rigor applied to truth-seeking, 128, 134–35
  trust dividend, 130–33
  truth and nothing but, 126–30
  truth-seeking questions, 160–61, 162
  See also alignment; trust-building in real time
truth-and-trust tactics. See alignment tactics
Twain, Mark, 180
Twitter, 102, 104–5, 112

U
Under Armour, 114
underperformance, 200–201
underperformers, 158–59, 168–70
Unilever, 73

V
values
  behaviors vs., 9
  and integrity, 115
  and work-life choice, 190–91
Van der Bergh, Rob, 5–6
variance analysis, 77, 84–86, 87–89
virtual employees. See telecommuters
VNU (Dutch conglomerate), 5–6. See also Nielsen
volunteering for hard duty, 203–4, 212

W
Wall Street Journal, 187, 191–92

water quality company, 7–8, 10–12

wedding gown retailer, 64, 70

Welch, Jack and Suzy

"Four Reasons to Quit Your Job," 177–78

"What I Wish I Knew at 21," 214

Winning, viii, 112, 125

"we're going to beat this" mentality, 28–29

WestJet Airlines, 50–51

whacks and wallops, 23–25, 32–33, 40–41

whack-recovery tactics

about, 25

get maniacal about the drivers of performance, 30–32

hang on tight to your best, 29–30

HDS story, 26–29, 31, 35–36

own your own whack, 27–29

reality-check your social architecture, 36–38

reinvent your strategy process, 32, 34–36

worry more productively, 38–40

"What I Wish I Knew at 21" (Welch and Welch), 214

Williams, Bunny, 71–72, 73, 189

wine business, European conglomerate in Napa Valley, 218–19

Winning (Welch and Welch), viii, 112, 125

win-win, globalization initiative as, 62–66

"Women in the Economy" conference (*Wall Street Journal*), 191–92

work

alignment as part of, 4

fun at work, 21–22, 125, 149–50

wow environment, 149–51

working capital turnover ratio and operating rate variance analysis, 86

work-life choice, 190–92, 193

worrying counterproductively, 159, 172

worrying productively, 38–40

"wow" team. *See* teambuilding

"wow" work environment, 149–51

Y

Yahoo, 163

"You Can Still Dunk in the Dark" ad campaign (Oreo), 104–5

YouGov's BrandIndex Buzz score, 117

Z

Zeliff, Michael, 165–67